IN DETAIL

House Design
MCINTURFF ARCHITECTS

IN DETAIL

House Design
McINTURFF ARCHITECTS

9

TEXT BY MARK McINTURFF • PHOTOGRAPHY BY JULIA HEINE • INTRODUCTION BY MICHAEL CROSBIE

First published in Australia in 2001 by
The Images Publishing Group Pty Ltd
ACN 059 734 431
6 Bastow Place, Mulgrave, Victoria 3170, Australia
Telephone: +(61 3) 9561 5544 Facsimile: +(61 3) 9561 4860
E-mail: books@images.com.au
Website: www.imagespublishing.com.au

Copyright © The Images Publishing Group Pty Ltd 2001
The Images Publishing Group Reference Number: 371

All rights reserved. Apart from any fair dealing for the purposes of private study, research, criticism or review as permitted under the Copyright Act, no part of this publication may be reproduced, stored in a retrieval system or transmitted in any form by any means, electronic, mechanical, photocopying, recording or otherwise, without the written permission of the publisher.

National Library of Australia Cataloguing-in-Publication Data

McInturff, Mark.
In detail: house design McInturff Architects.

Bibliography.
Includes index.
ISBN 1 86470 100 5.

1. McInturff Architects. 2. Architecture, Domestic – United States. 3. Dwellings – Remodeling – United States. 4. Architecture – United States – Details. I. McInturff Architects. II. Title. (Series: House design; 9).

728.0973

Designed by The Graphic Image Studio Pty Ltd
Mulgrave, Australia

Film by Rainbow Graphics & Printing Co., Ltd.

Printed by Paramount Printing Co. Ltd., Hong Kong

CONTENTS

6 Introduction

Selected Projects
8 Denning Residence
12 Private Residence
20 King Stair
22 Knight Residence III
30 Couch Weekend House
38 Feller Residence
42 Hutner Residence
46 Borsecnik Weil Residence
52 House in the Woods
58 Heard Teng Residence II
64 Armstrong House
72 Residence in Old Town
80 Hanson Sciannella Residence
86 Weiner Residence II
92 Withers House
98 Cozzens Residence
106 Martin Shocket Residence

Selected Works
114 McInturff House + Studio
114 Jakob Residence
115 Knight Weekend House
115 Taylor Residence II
116 Spring Valley Residence
116 Feffer Yingling Beach House
117 Harth Residence
117 Andrews Viudez Residence + Studio
118 Sigma Nu Fraternity House, George Washington University
118 O'Connor Beach House
119 Bartlett Ignani Residence
119 Bronstein Cohen Library
120 Tasker House
120 Apartment House in Washington DC
121 Raff House
121 Addition to a Virginia Farm

123 **Firm Profile**

124 **Works and Credits**

126 **Selected Bibliography**

127 **Acknowledgments**

128 **Index**

INTRODUCTION

In the world of architecture house additions, renovations, and projects on small sites wedged into existing neighborhoods are considered the types of projects that one just starting his or her own practice must inevitably pass through on the way to something grander and greater. Frank Lloyd Wright moonlighted while practicing with Adler & Sullivan, doing small domestic projects for family and friends, and many of today's celebrated architects took much the same path. The assumption is that small, residential projects are a rite of passage that lead to the work that one really became an architect for: the high profile museum, the office tower, the prestigious university building.

What we as architects often forget, or never realize, is that there is architectural greatness to be had in the simple commission, and it is at this scale, in fact, where most architects fall in love. It is only later, after we have moved on to the so-called bigger and better commissions, that we wish we could be working again on those small-scale projects, on which we could lavish our attention and time as designers. This is why we became architects.

Talk to Mark McInturff about his work and you will immediately recognize a man still in love with architecture. Over the past 15 years, since founding his own firm on the Maryland outskirts of Washington, D.C., McInturff has purposely kept his firm small—about a half-dozen people, many of whom have been with the firm for years. This is a close-knit group with lots of collaboration on projects. This allows McInturff, as a principal, to stay intimately involved with designing and building. It also means that he spends less time beating the bushes for work to "feed the monster," and running a business. The majority of the firm's work is still residential-new houses, renovations, additions-and some modest commercial and institutional projects. At this scale McInturff can maintain a comfortable level of control on all the projects in his office and be intimately involved at every level-from the large conceptual vision of the design to the diminutive details of how a beam and a post come together, or the profile of a window casing, or the nosing on a stair. Looking through this book, one can see how much pleasure McInturff and his collaborators still take in the practice of architecture ("pleasure" in this case includes generous measures of both agony and ecstasy to bring one's designs to reality).

McInturff is also very judicious about where he works. Although he has completed projects in other parts of the country, he enjoys most working in his own backyard of suburban Washington, Maryland, and Virginia. This reduces the amount of time it takes to be on-site at one of his projects, and makes it easier to be there when critical points in a project happen—just framing the envelope and roughing in windows and doors, or laying out an outdoor space, or working out the texture of a concrete finish. Before he was an architect, McInturff worked as a carpenter (for a time swinging a hammer at Paolo Soleri's Cosanti in Arizona). The thrill of creation— when people bring drawings and materials together on site to birth a work of architecture— is at the core of being an architect for McInturff. Here is where the real magic happens. The drawings provide a starting point and the refinements may be worked out on the building site, in all their terrific and terrifying splendor. McInturff describes this experience as truly moving (like that of a dad in a delivery room), seeing the fruition of a design that his clients have been good enough, and trusting enough, to allow him to build. It is also the only time when an architect can adjust those design hunches described in a roll of drawings to be more fully faithful to the image he sees in his head. Miss its birth on site, and the opportunity to fine-tune it is forever lost.

McInturff's heroes are those architects who exhibit the fine-grained attention to design detail that he loves. Carlo Scarpa, Mies van der Rohe, Louis Kahn—all of these architects understood that God (or the devil, depending on your denomination) is in the details. Another architect that McInturff admires, Charles Moore, was not noted for his details, but for his ability to draw from people their dreams and secret wishes, upon which he embroidered his designs. McInturff studied with Moore, traveled with him, and discovered that architectural wonder can be created almost anywhere. This is why houses continue to be his choice work. Houses involve a level of emotional investment from the client that is missing in many other building types. These are meaningful structures to the people who will live there, and McInturff welcomes them as part of the creative process.

Having long worked in the realm of renovations and additions, McInturff approaches architecture with a complexity and complicity that architects used to working on clean slates might envy. McInturff does not believe in the "seamless" addition, where the new architect's work should disappear within the language of the older building. In any project, McInturff explores its underlying order. He attempts to draw what is interesting out of what is there, taking that as a starting point upon which to base his own design. This might range from the stylistic language of the older building or its materials, to its scale, or its relation to the outdoors, or the hierarchy between public and private spaces. It might recall the history of a place, or it might draw together the disparate pieces of many structures built over time (as in his own house and studio in Bethesda, Maryland). But many times what's there to start with is not much in terms of architectural quality or interest. It then becomes the architect's mission to create something interesting and engaging out of virtually nothing. McInturff's challenge is to do this while not ignoring what is there—to create a new environment that stands on its own, architecturally, while not undermining the context. It is a delicate balancing art, and it demands an attention and sensitivity to detail that is the product of years of practice.

For example, in the Borsecnik Weil residence, McInturff celebrates the existing building's lukewarm modernism by turning up the stylistic volume. The addition is a clean, crisp, light-filled ode to modernism that is faithful to the old 1950s house while providing a fresh interpretation of its architectural language. It pays homage to the old, but takes center stage all the same.

In another case, the Feller residence, the existing house and its site yielded an opportunity to create a new outdoor space inside, mediating between house and garden. Again, the response is just right for the circumstances and melds inside and outside.

Outdoor spaces are abundant in McInturff's work. He attributes the roots of this interest to Moore and European design, and practices in a climate in which shady garden spaces are a welcome respite in the summer humidity that Washington is infamous for. McInturff's designs are for outdoor rooms, gracious garden spaces that are usually extensions of the home's interior. One of the best examples is the Heard Teng II residence, in which green space, water, paving, and an arbor echo an interior arrangement of rooms that offer excellent vantages of the garden. Another project, the Weiner II residence, is an exercise in preserving and tending a tiny outdoor space of only 200 square feet in the rear of the home. The new dwelling is a cozy combination of two homes that sit adjacent to each other, with many of the interior spaces borrowing light or views from the postage-stamp back yard. In this case, the outdoor space is not only an amenity, but provides the critical access to light and air that make viable this combination of two homes into one.

Any one of the projects in this book reveals McInturff's infatuation with details. The beams and columns in the Andrews Viudez residence and studio are an exercise in structure as sculpture. The Bronstein Cohn library suggests the intimately scaled and richly detailed spaces of Wright's own house and studio in Oak Park, Illinois. The cladding of the Tasker house demonstrates a range of scale and depth that can be achieved with relatively simple, vernacular materials. The King Stair is a detailing tour de force that articulates every connection between one floor and the next. The Withers house takes common materials such as asphalt shingles and corrugated sheet metal, and uses them in ways that turn a cabin in the woods into a miniature art museum.

Mark McInturff's choice to keep his practice small and personally manageable has preserved for him those very aspects of architecture that attracts us to it. For young architecture students looking forward to that day when their dreams will become built reality, and for older architects looking backward from the lofty peaks of principaldom where one's designs can be recognized only in their broadest conceptual outlines, McInturff's architecture reminds all of us that the joy of architecture is in the journey, and in the very parts we can grasp with our hands.

Michael J. Crosbie
Essex, Connecticut

SELECTED PROJECTS

DENNING RESIDENCE

Washington DC, USA
Completion: 1991

1 Axonometric
Opposite:
Kitchen

In 1970, architect Roger Lewis built six speculative cooperative tower houses in northwest Washington DC. The multi-level houses, grouped around a common parking court, were simply built in terms of detail but had good bones, including a split section that allowed for interlocking spaces and a double-height living room. The rules of the cooperative require that a general similarity be maintained on the outside, but allow considerable variation within.

Our client asked us to elaborate on the simple drywall interior. Little was changed in terms of volume or square footage, but much was added through the addition of materials. To order and shape the existing plan, a new architecture was inserted into the original volumes—an architecture of wood, aluminum, stone, and fiber, a sensuous architecture of warm and cool, hard and soft, reflective and translucent.

Triangular maple columns with aluminum reveals, internally lit and topped by rice paper tubes, define the entry area and set off the living room; maple piers along the wall support a system of aluminum shelves. The columns maintain a constant height as they continue up the stairs and mark the boundary of the new kitchen, which has custom-maple cabinets, also with aluminum reveals. A curved wall carrying a pair of sandblasted glass doors separates the dining room from the kitchen. The kitchen, dining room, and living room are linked by an axis marked overhead by a dropped ceiling plane, which supports a 16-foot V-shaped light fixture made of aluminum and translucent rice paper-like fiber. This axis ends in the living room, where the existing windows are framed in a new blue wall plane. The large window openings can be covered in a variety of configurations by a system of sliding panels, steel framed, and covered in the same translucent fiber.

On the exterior wall parallel to the circulation and stair route, two slender triangular bay windows project into the trees beyond. The removal of much of the original wall between adjacent runs opens the stair to itself, and a tall, slender window that climbs four levels with the stair opens it to the trees.

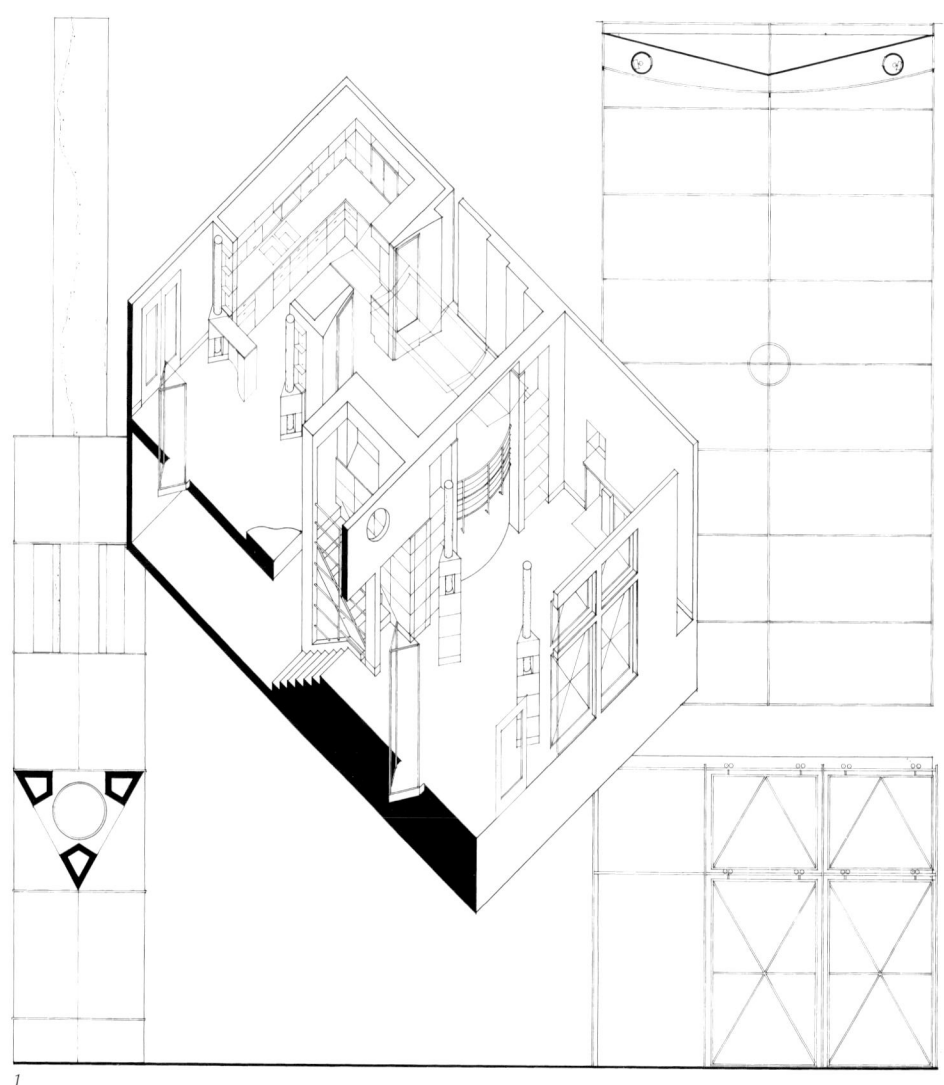

1

8 | DENNING RESIDENCE

3

4

5

3&5 Living room
4 View toward entry
6 Column detail
7 Plan

PRIVATE RESIDENCE

Washington DC, USA
Completion: 1993

1

Located at an acute angle of two busy in-town commuter routes, this house has views across a reservoir to the Potomac River and beyond. The extreme contrasts of busy traffic and expansive natural views have generated a form for the complete renovation of an ordinary 1950s era house.

This one-bedroom house is a highly particular response to site, client, and program. In taking a more protective attitude against the street, the existing gambrel/mansard roof has been subsumed into a thick façade that swells at the center to provide a more generous entry. The focus of this entry, and now the entire house, is the stair, which has been reconfigured and detailed to allow light to reach from a second floor skylight down to the main level. The stair occupies a glass cube, which serves to contain the energy of its movements and to separate it from the loft-like first floor, now structurally opened up to provide the scale of space necessary to view the owner's ever-growing collection of modern art.

The polygonal room oriented toward the acute angle of the site has been converted from the dining room to the kitchen. Above, a new library takes advantage of its position and view. These two tower spaces are vertically connected by light, penetrating first through the library roof, then through a glass-topped table to the kitchen below. Outside, this tower marks the confluence of the two roads and acknowledges the similar form of a classically domed reservoir pump building across the way.

A consistent language of detail has been used throughout, involving brushed stainless steel, painted steel, limed oak, and glass. This palette, used in the design of the stair and rails, the glass walls, and the display shelving, delicately tie together these spaces while providing an appropriate setting for the art. The kitchen and dining room tables and the exterior and library light fixtures, designed by the architect, incorporate these same materials.

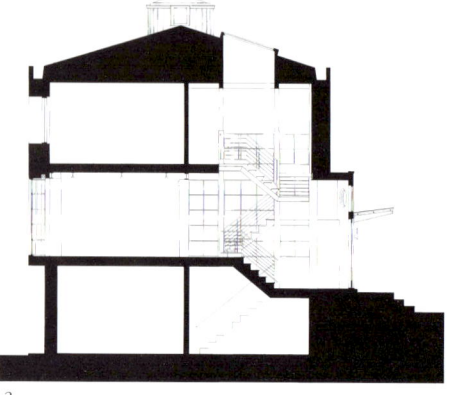
2

1 Entry façade
2 Section through entry and stair
3 Axonometric
Opposite:
   Tower detail

3

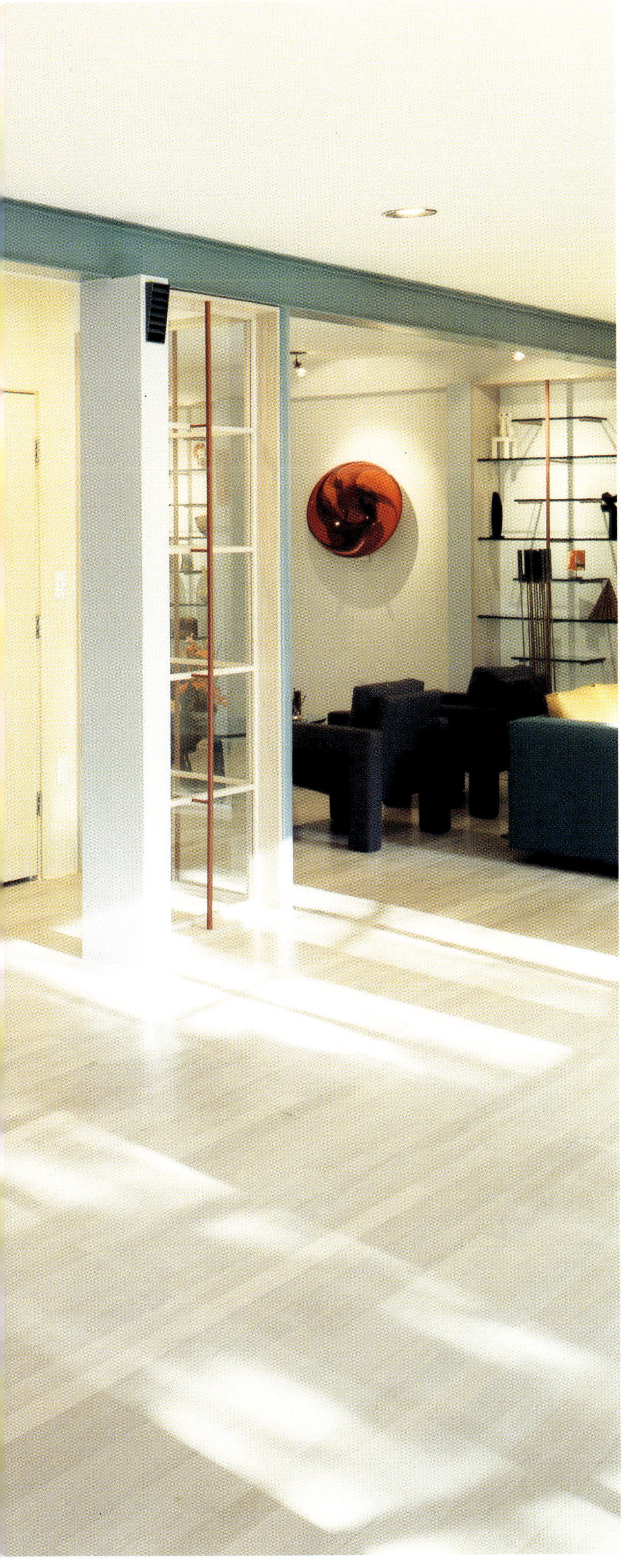

6

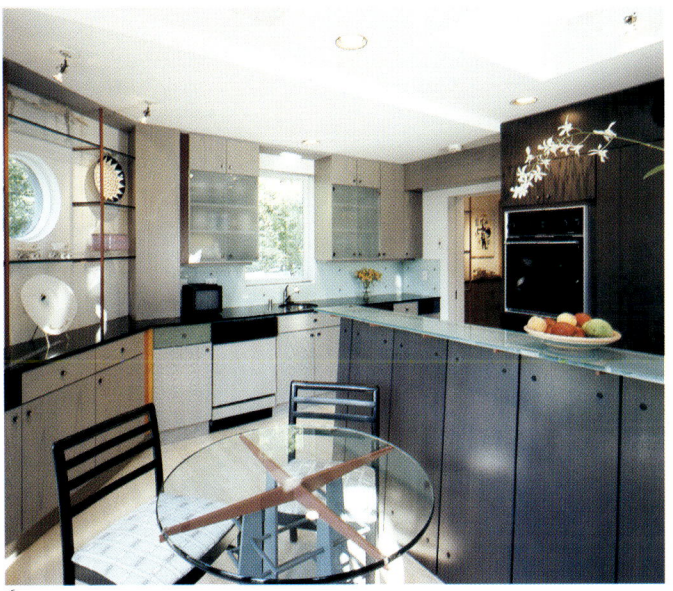

5 View of living room from dining room
6 Kitchen

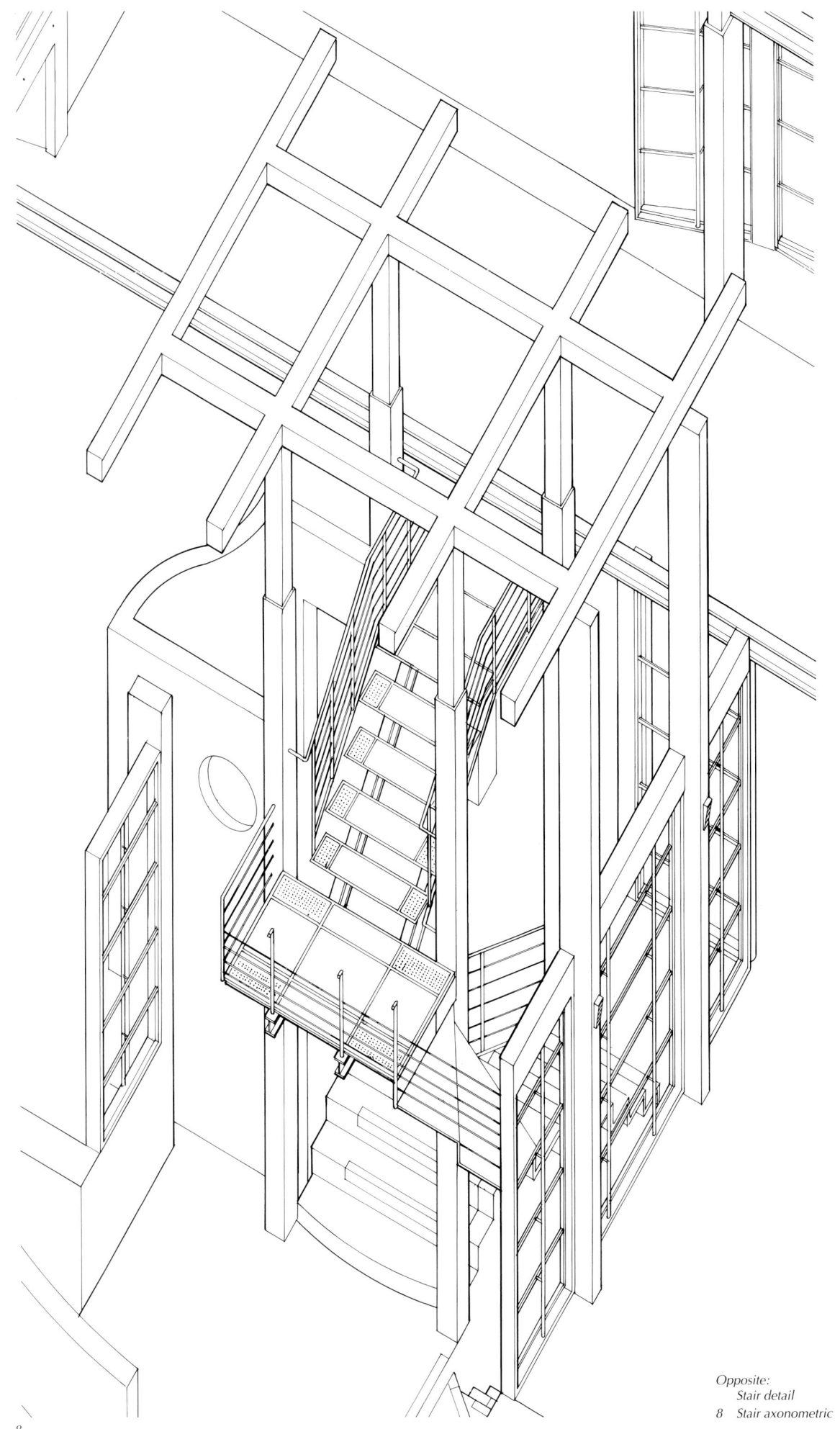

Opposite:
Stair detail
8   Stair axonometric

First Floor/Before

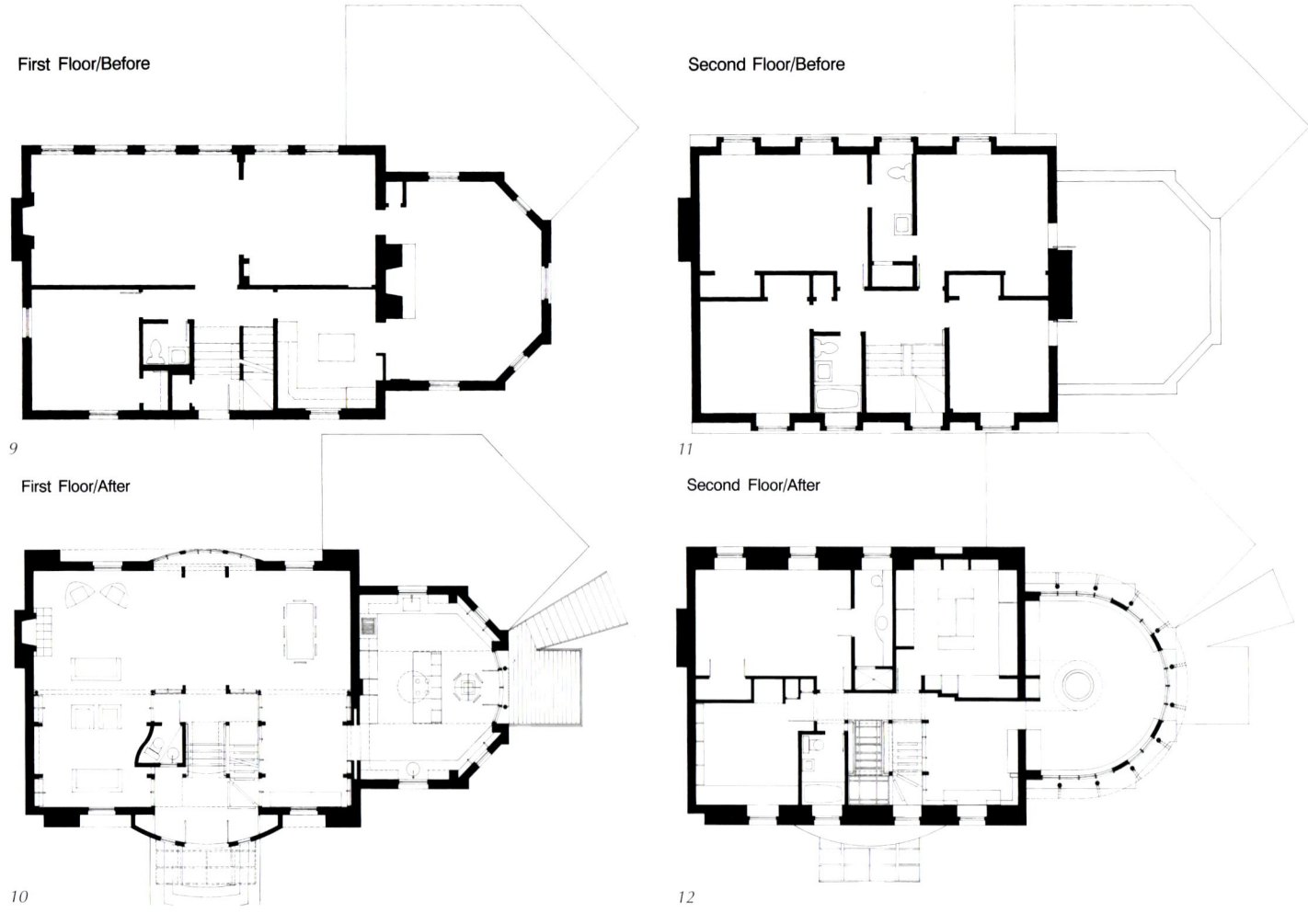

9

First Floor/After

10

Second Floor/Before

11

Second Floor/After

12

13

18 | PRIVATE RESIDENCE

9 & 11 Plans, before
10 & 12 Plans, after
13 Stair and entry
14 Stair above entry

14

KING STAIR

Chevy Chase, Maryland, USA
Completion: 1994

3

The addition of a new third floor to a 1920's house also provided the opportunity for a new stair.

We took this to be both literally and figuratively the center of the house, and designed the new piece to reflect the transition from the traditional forms of the original space to the more modern aesthetic of the new ones. Starting opposite the front door only the railing design hints at what follows. At the second floor landing, the solidity of the lower run gives way to an open stair, detailed with a minimalist profile and open risers to allow light from above to penetrate the stair and light the entry below. Wooden plank treads join with steel rods, channels, and cables to create a visual and tactile contrast.

At the top landing, these planks continue as a cantilevered gallery to provide access to new third floor rooms. Gaps between the boards, between landing and wall, and between stair treads allow light to filter below and help articulate the pieces of this 'kit-of-parts' approach.

1 Third floor landing
2 Tread detail
3 Detail of connections
Opposite:
   Second floor landing

1

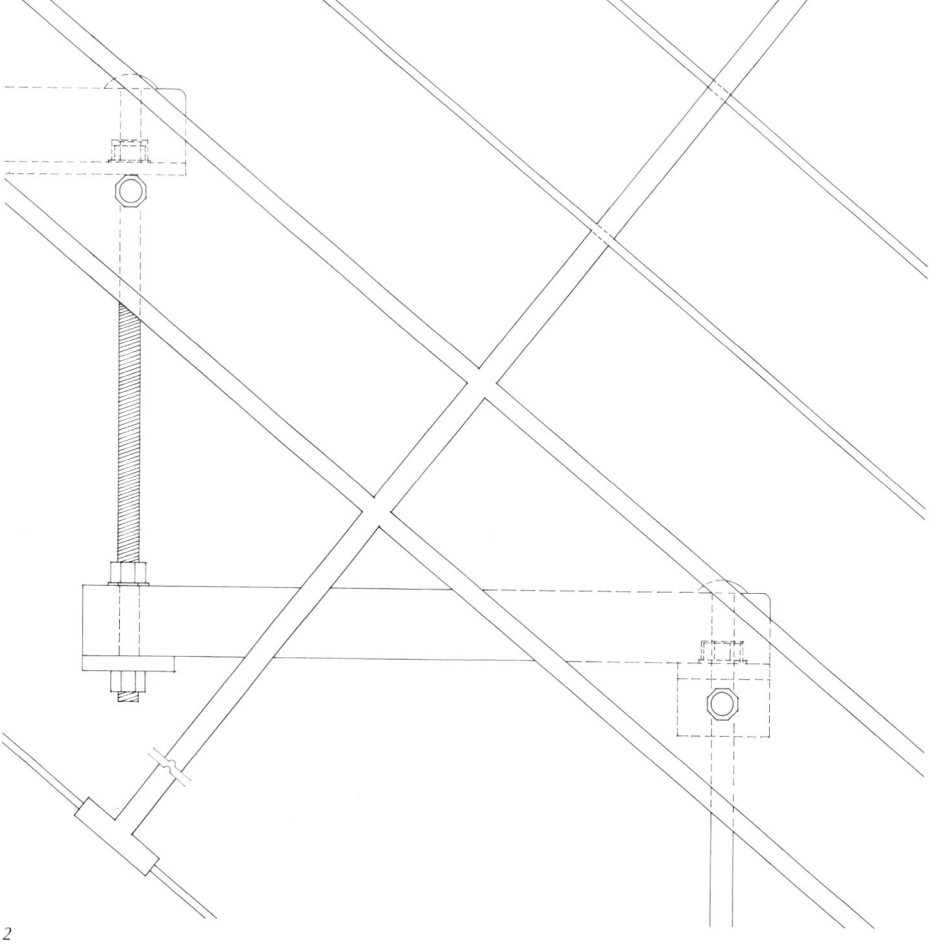

2

KNIGHT RESIDENCE III

Chevy Chase, Maryland, USA
Completion: 1994

Situated on a sloped wooded site overlooking Rock Creek Park, between two 1950s modern houses by architect Charles Goodman, this small house attempts to reconcile a modest budget with a desire for expansive, light-filled spaces. The house, configured to accommodate the mature trees found on the site, is broken into three parts: a carport; a simply and rationally built 16-foot-wide bar, containing library and kitchen on the main level, bedrooms and bathrooms below, and master suite above; and the barrel-vaulted volume containing living and dining. A line of 14 reinforced concrete columns, angled relative to the rest of the plan, links all three pieces. This line energizes the geometry of the house and forces the perspective of the hall, ending at a small pool whose jets mask the sounds of the parkway beyond.

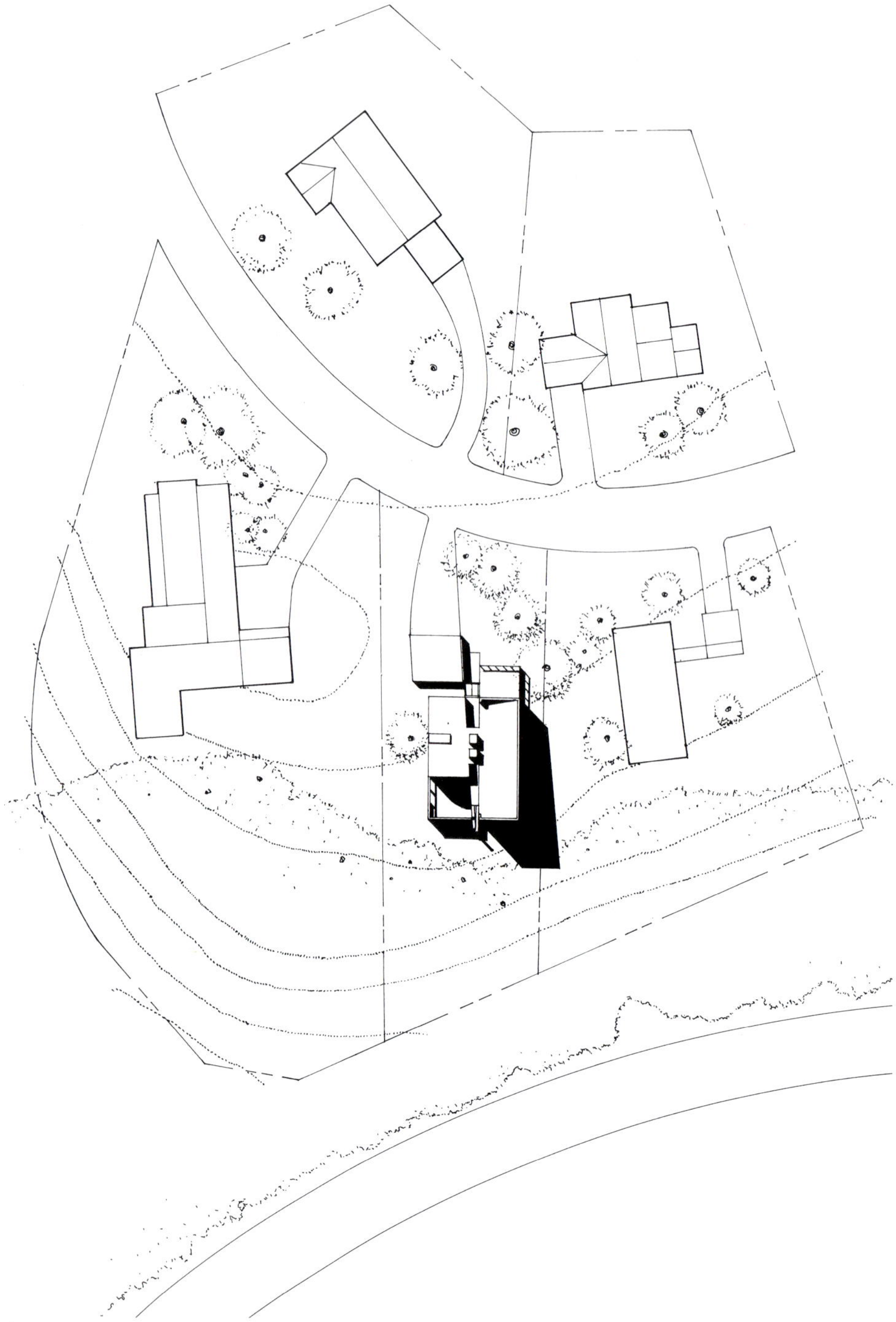

The owners, for whom the architect had worked twice before, now have grown children. The guest bedrooms, tucked under the main level, free up the remainder of the house to be a generous open plan for the two inhabitants.

Materials were chosen for their economy—plywood, metal, concrete—as well as for their expressive possibilities. Post and beam framing, corrugated metal, and white rooms accented by rich colors are favored elements from a weekend house designed and built several years ago by this team of architect and clients, and reappear here, bringing the light-filled generous spaces of their weekends into their daily city life.

1   Entry façade
2   Site plan
Opposite:
   Façade facing wooded parkland

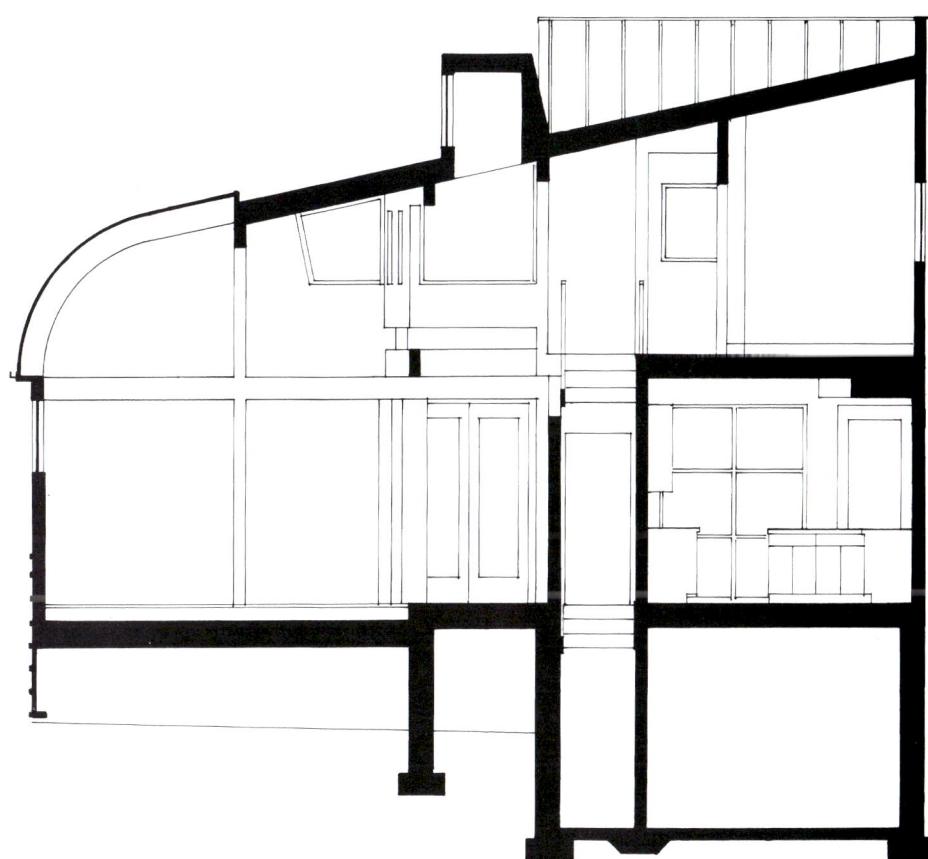

4　Night view
5　Section
6　Kitchen

McInturff Architects | 25

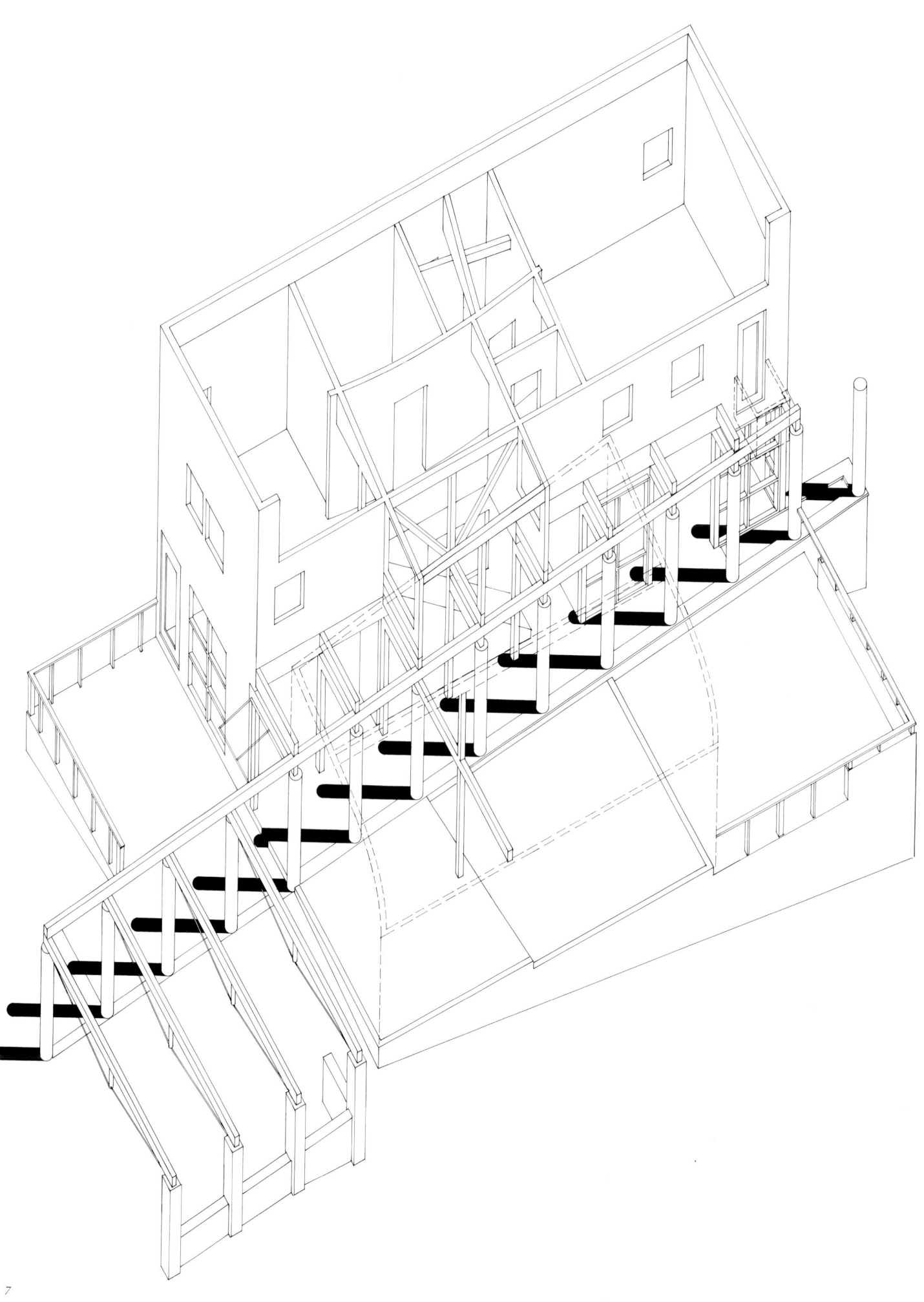

7

7   Axonometric
8   View from library toward entry
9   Living room and colonnade from entry

McInturff Architects | 27

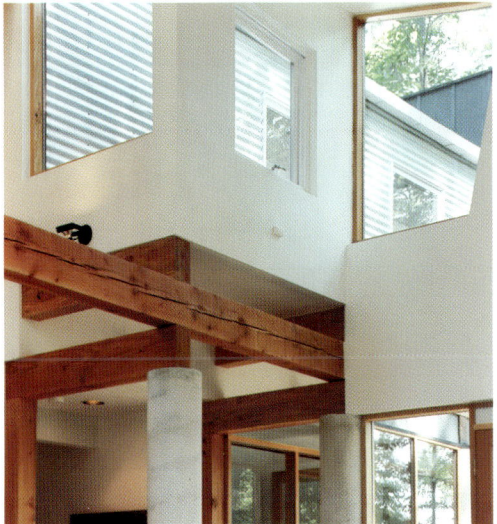

Opposite:
Column detail with stair beyond
11 Corner detail
12 Second floor plan and section

11

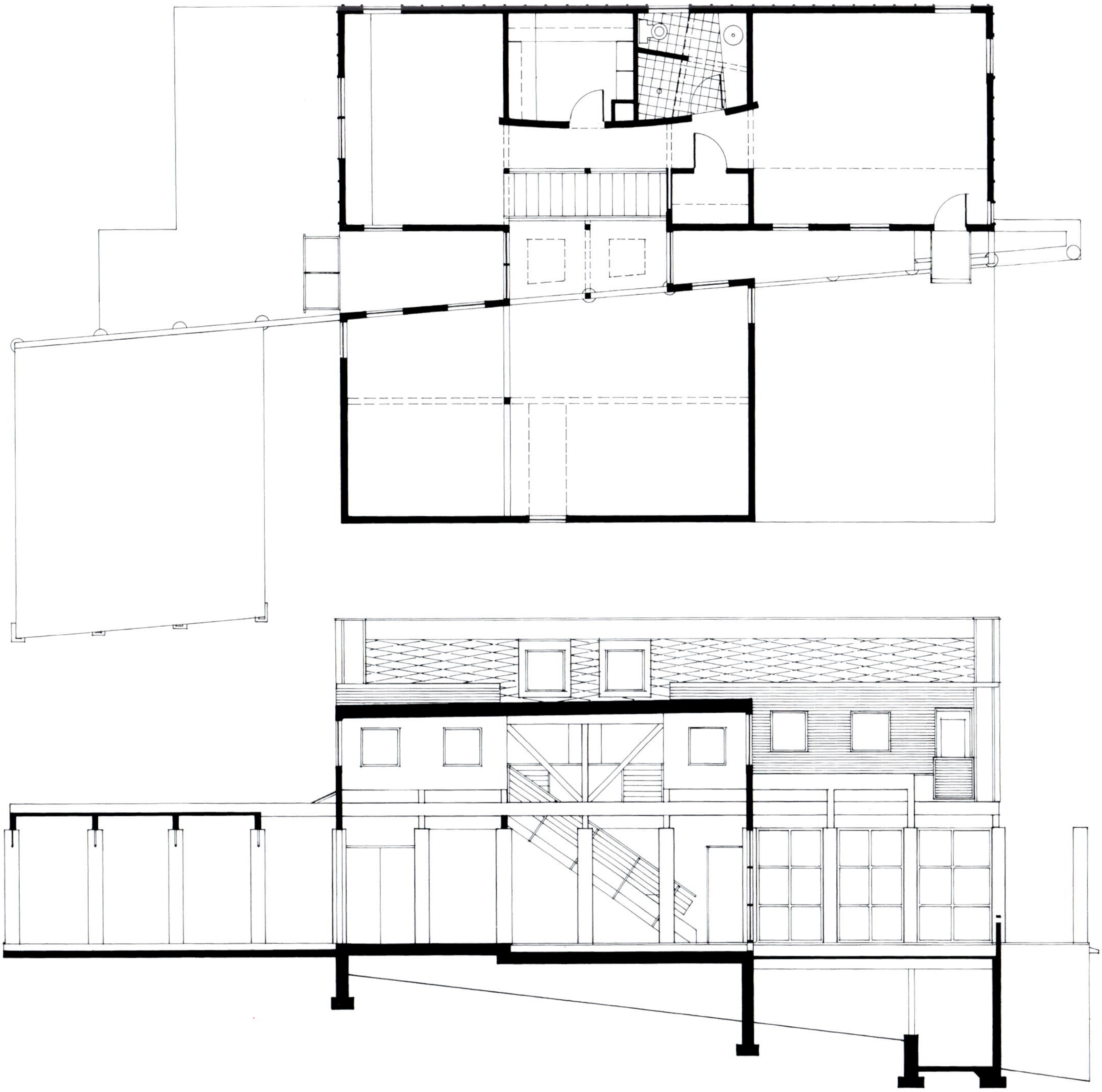

12

COUCH WEEKEND HOUSE

Hampshire County, West Virginia, USA
Completion: 1995

1

This tiny, 1,000-square-foot house sits high on a wooded cliff in West Virginia, overlooking the Cacapon River some 300 feet below.

Sited and organized to take advantage of this extraordinary panorama, the house is divided into three separate buildings: the domestic rooms for sitting, cooking, and sleeping, a work room/studio, and a tower of porches. The owner requested that the interiors of these spaces be spartan, almost monastic, with little furniture; the primary seating is provided by floor cushions and the ledge created by the two-level living room. The simple detailing of the interior is enhanced by the use of old barn beams, which were recycled to provide interior posts, beams, railings, and mantle.

Outdoor walks and bridges functionally connect the three buildings, while they are structurally connected by an 80-foot stone wall that follows the ridgeline and supports part of each building. The wall—part mountain, ruin, and house—appears to have always been there, while the three little houses seem temporary but familiar visitors to this profoundly beautiful site.

1 Model
2 Entry façade
Opposite:
  View from downhill

2

30 | COUCH WEEKEND HOUSE

4 View of mountains from tower
5 View from tower
6 Tower side façade
7 Elevations and site section

4

5

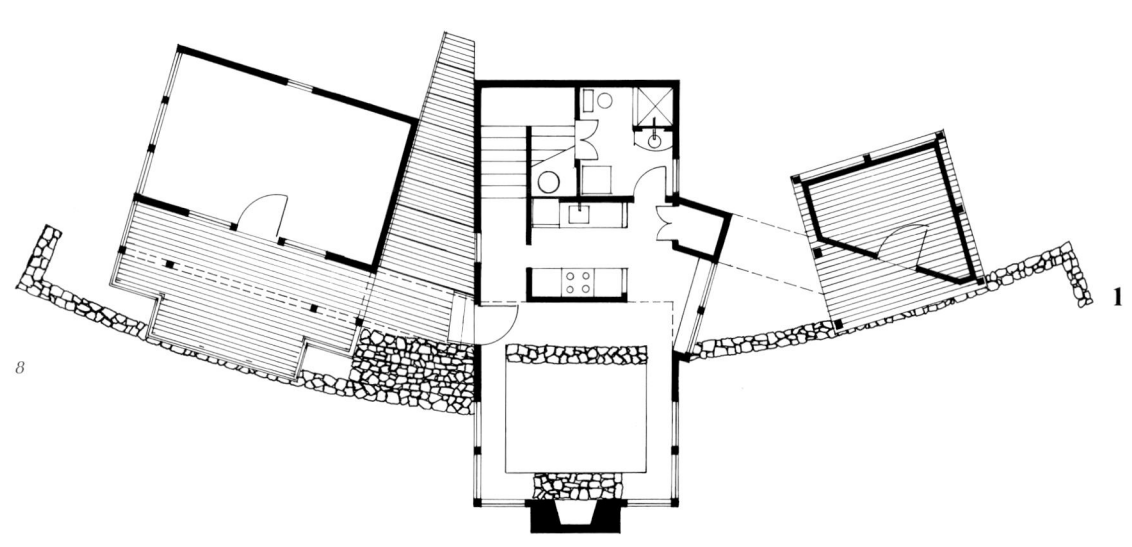
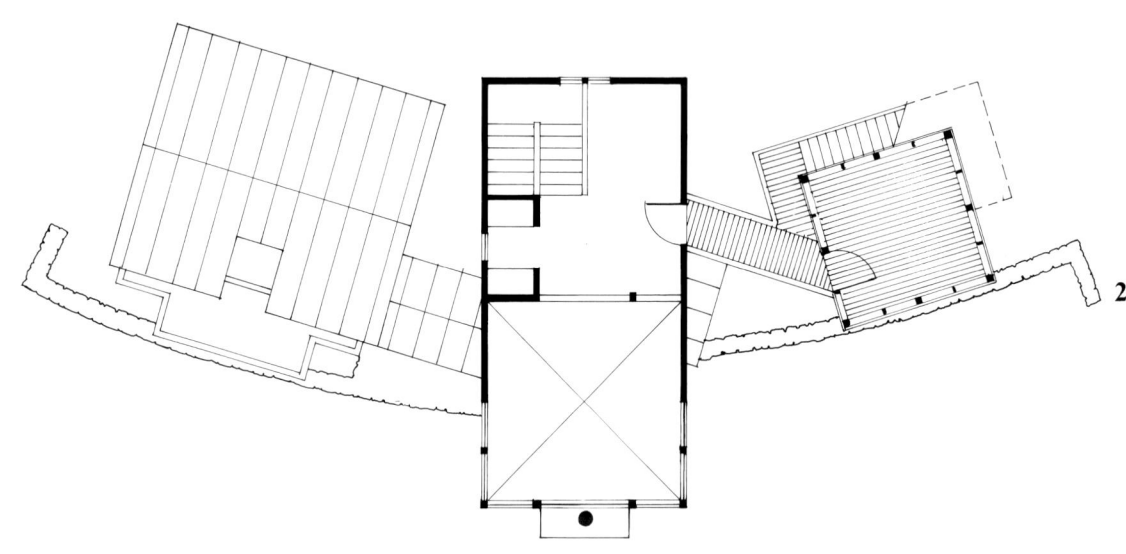
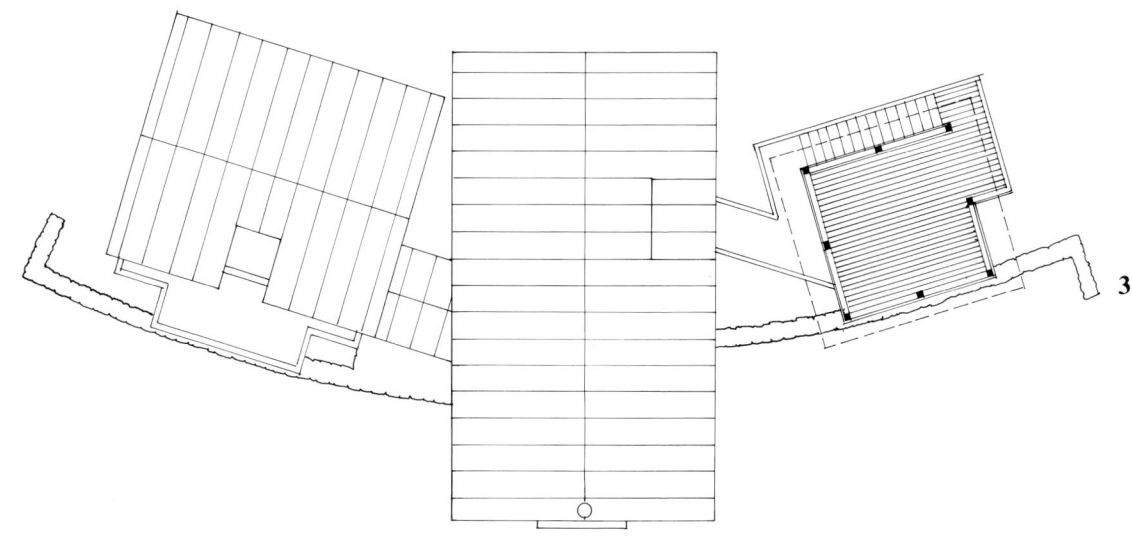

8 Plans
Opposite:
   Living room

34 | COUCH WEEKEND HOUSE

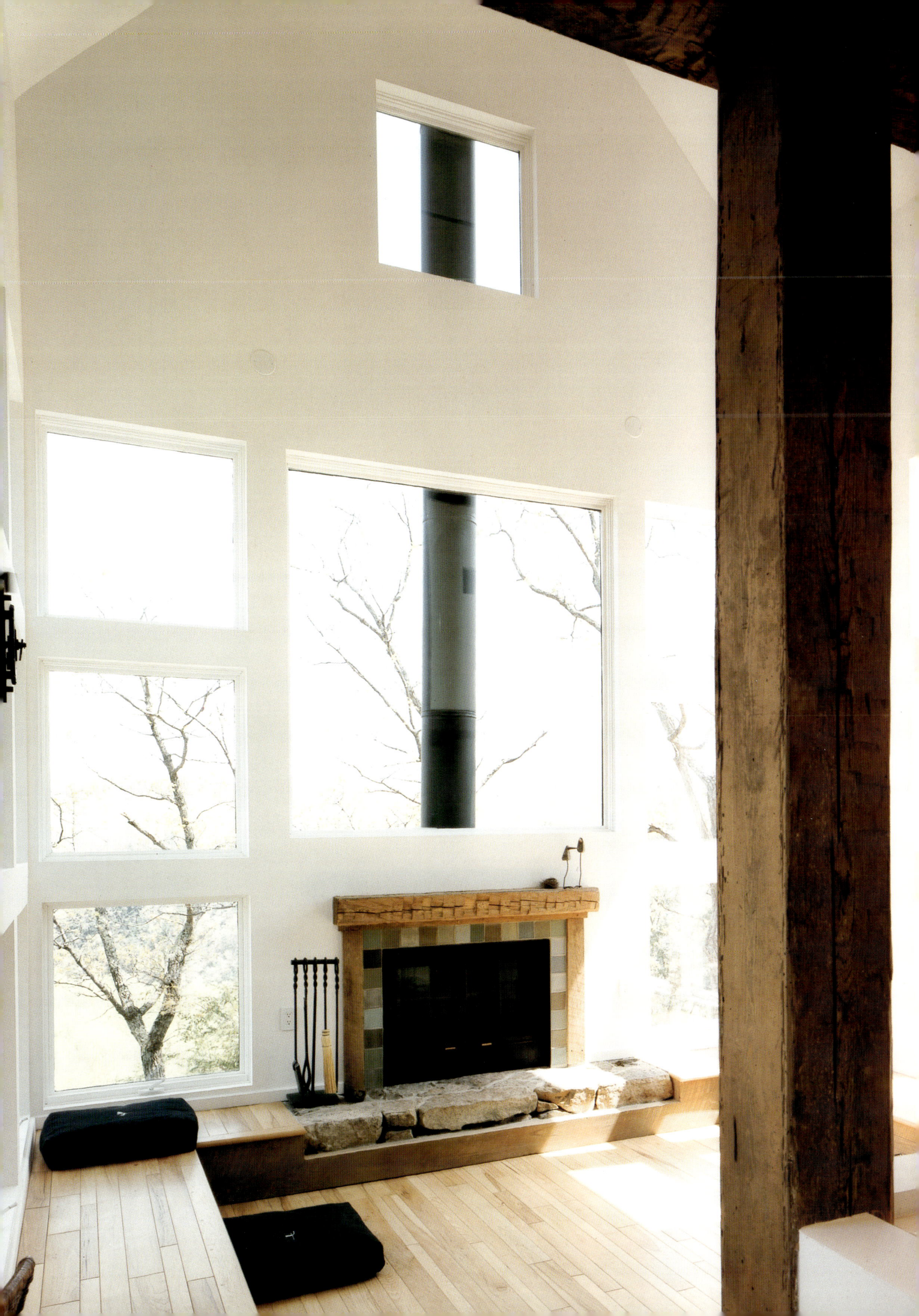

10

10 View from studio porch
11 View of house from across valley
12 Tower stair
13 Elevations

McInturff Architects | 37

FELLER RESIDENCE

Washington DC, USA
Completion: 1995

This project adds to a 1920s foursquare Washington house—not by extending the existing structure and vocabulary of the house, but by building a garden.

In order to define a new outdoor room, five freestanding stucco walls and a canopy of steel and glass have been juxtaposed. Placement of each of these elements was determined by the existing relationships of house to site. The walls terminate views and axes extending from the house; they screen views of a truncated carport and a dog run; and they enclose a paved courtyard. The largest wall was punctured with uniform openings through which a glass box weaves, enclosing a piece of the new garden as an interior room. Within this room, specific functions were fixed only by a fireplace and a built-in table; the latter inhabits a glass bay, which projects beyond the boundaries of the original house and allows views across the Potomac River to Virginia.

Detailing is spare throughout, with finishes that connect interior and exterior—limestone paving, stucco, steel, and glass. These materials extend further into the house and the new kitchen.

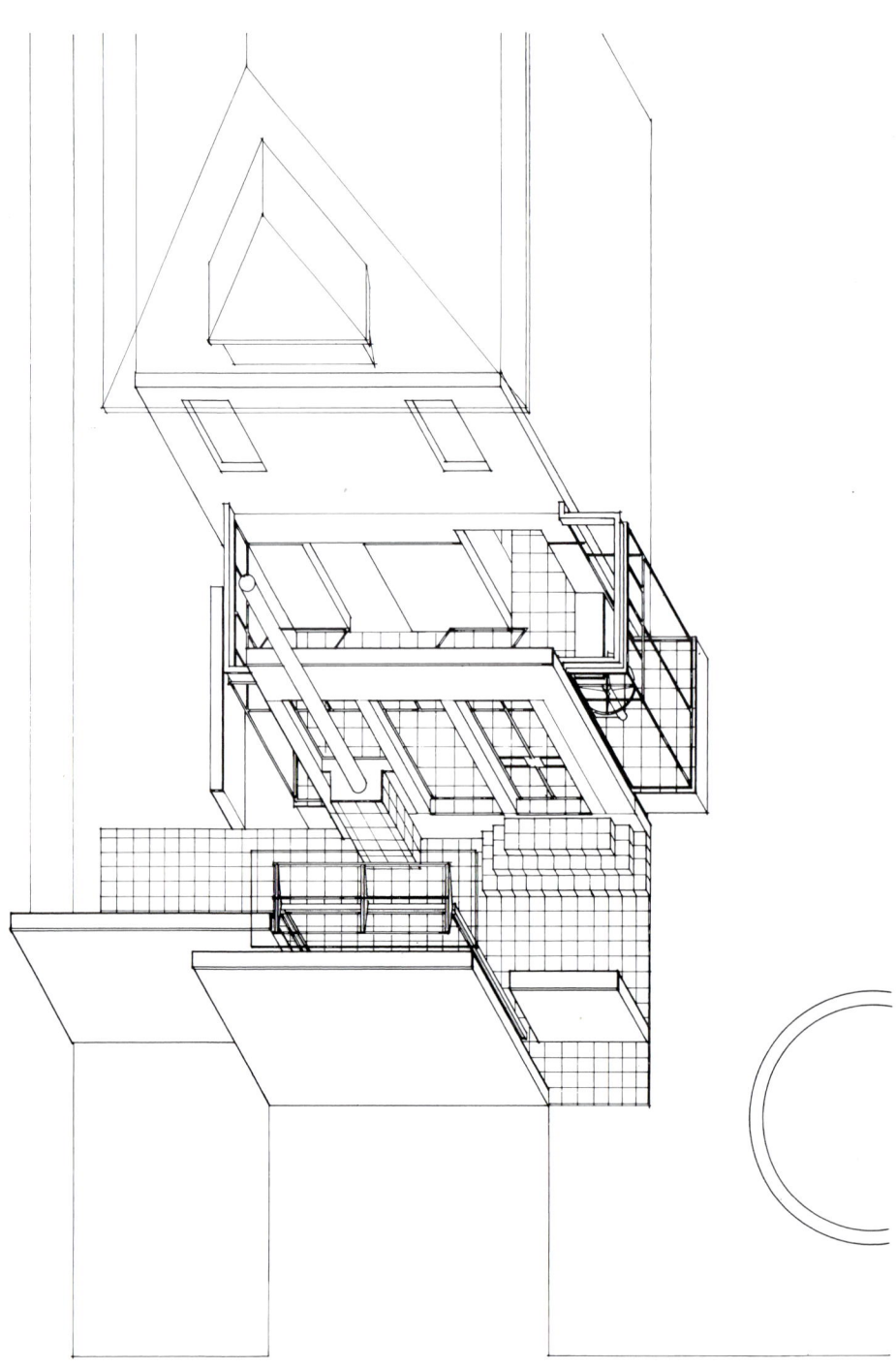

1 New garden room
2 Axonometric
Opposite:
   New garden room with original house beyond

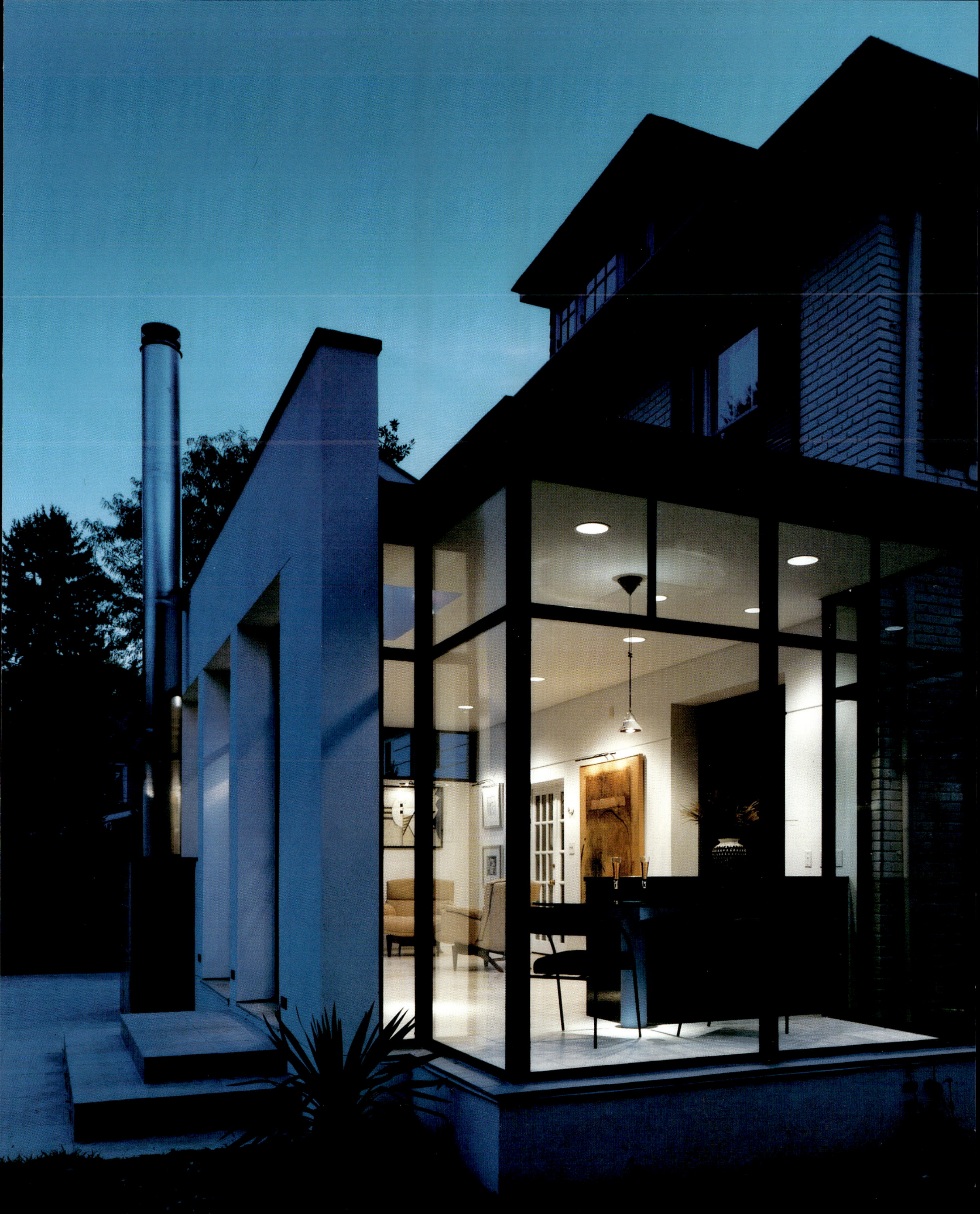

4

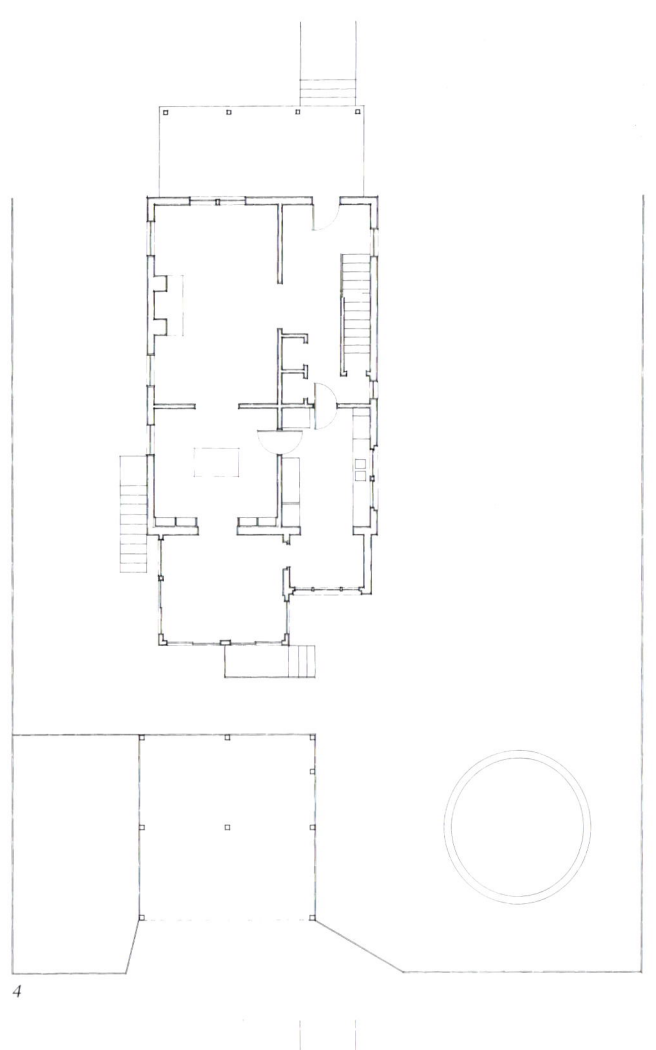

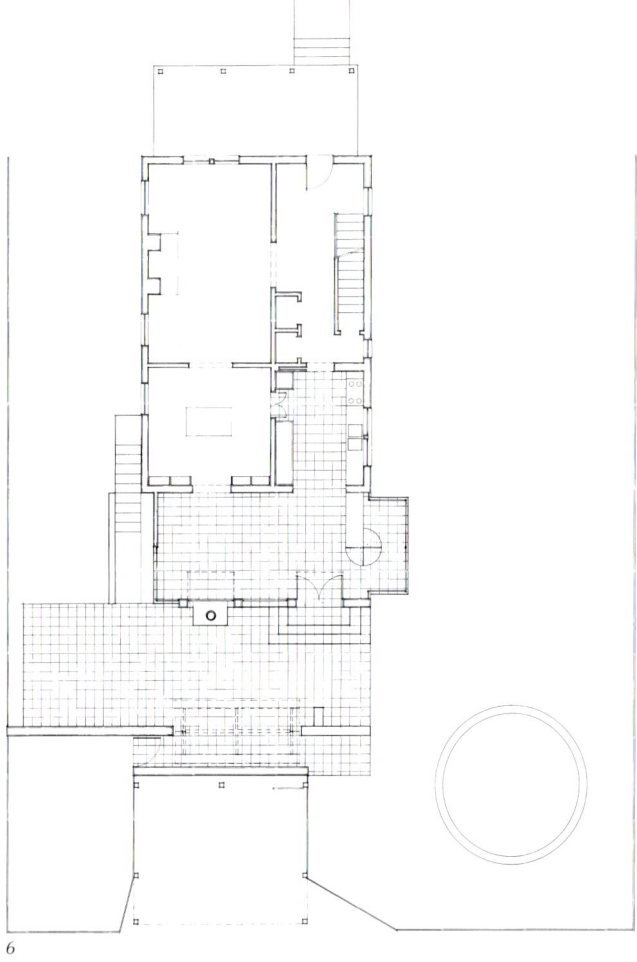

5

6

7

40 | FELLER RESIDENCE

8

9

4 Plan, before
5 Courtyard view
6 Plan, after
7 Kitchen view, looking toward fountain
8 Garden elevation
9 Garden room entry

McInturff Architects | 41

HUTNER RESIDENCE

Chevy Chase, Maryland, USA
Completion: 1995

This renovation and addition attempt to bring order and a sense of spaciousness to a tiny postwar rambler, whose original, vaguely H-shaped plan had been a warren of small, dark rooms. To this end, the middle of the 'H' has been removed entirely, and a new two-story center inserted, whose roofline continues that of the existing wings. On the first floor a living/music room and a family/television room can open or close to one another via a series of French doors, accommodating a variety of uses. Although the new plan is simplified, interest is added through detailing, with the dividing wall and the new stair as carefully crafted centerpieces. Above, the new second floor includes a master bedroom, bath and study, connected ensuite to allow the overall space to read around a blue-painted service core.

In the end, this is still a small house, but one made to feel generous through the flexible-use open plan, borrowed space, and variety in detailing and materials.

1 Front façade
2 Living room
3 Family room with stair to new second story

4

5

6

7

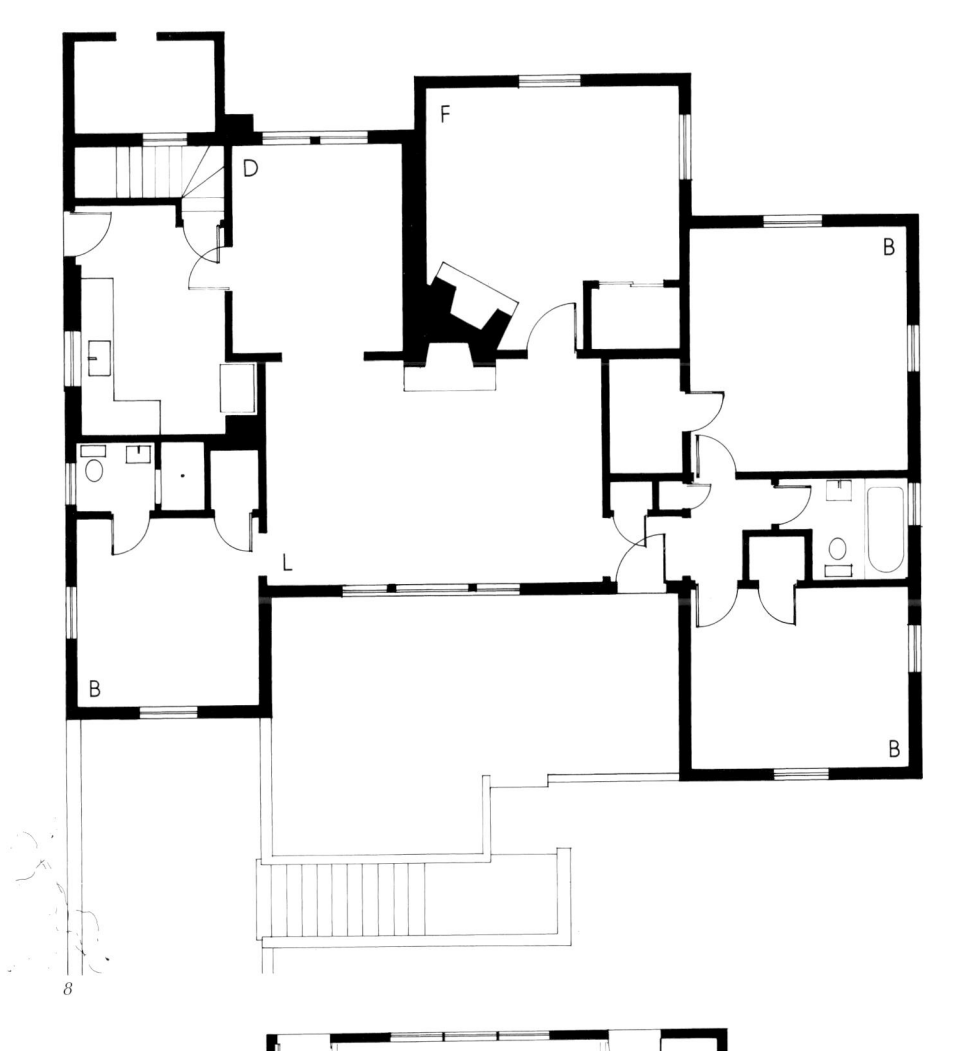

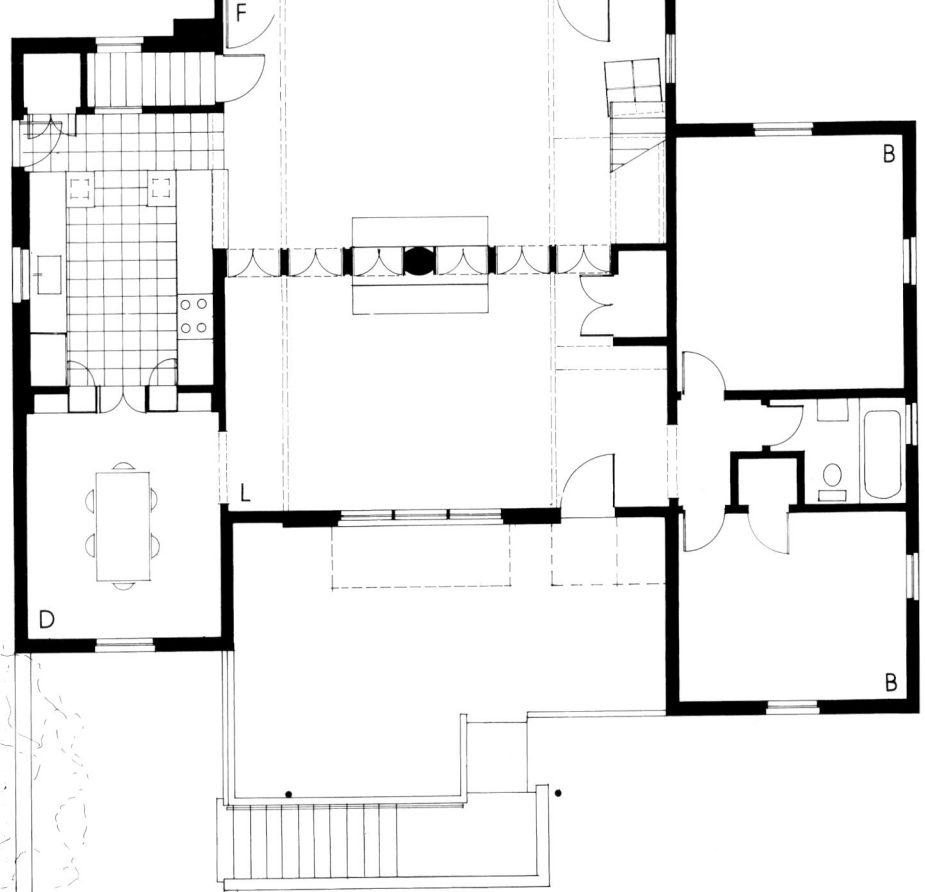

4   Stair
5   Kitchen
6   Master bathroom
7   Entry with stair landing above
8   First floor plan, before
9   First floor plan, after

McInturff Architects | 45

BORSECNIK WEIL RESIDENCE

Chevy Chase, Maryland, USA
Completion: 1996

Our clients bought a small one-story 1950s house in an established Washington suburb that exhibited the tentative modern spirit then emerging in Washington-area domestic architecture—an idea since gone into hiding. The original long, light-filled living room opening to a garden was quite fine, but the organization of the remaining plan confused public and private realms, creating a rabbit warren of dark spaces. Broad overhangs and a V-shaped corner column had a dynamic that still rang true, but the brooding quality and clumsiness of other elements did not agree with the incipient modern spirit found in the basic form.

To clarify organization, the existing horizontal roof plane was complemented by a yellow wall slicing through the house, inside and out, bisecting the plan and forming four spatial quadrants. Public rooms are on one side and private on the other; the new stair hall crosses between the zones.

Removing one first floor bedroom allowed for a larger kitchen, and living and dining areas were combined into a larger, more open space. A new V-shaped column between living and dining areas, the yellow wall, and large expanses of horizontally mullioned windows help unite interior and exterior in ways the original house had only begun to realize.

1   Street elevation
2   Façade detail
Opposite:
    Stair hall

46 | BORSECNIK WEIL RESIDENCE

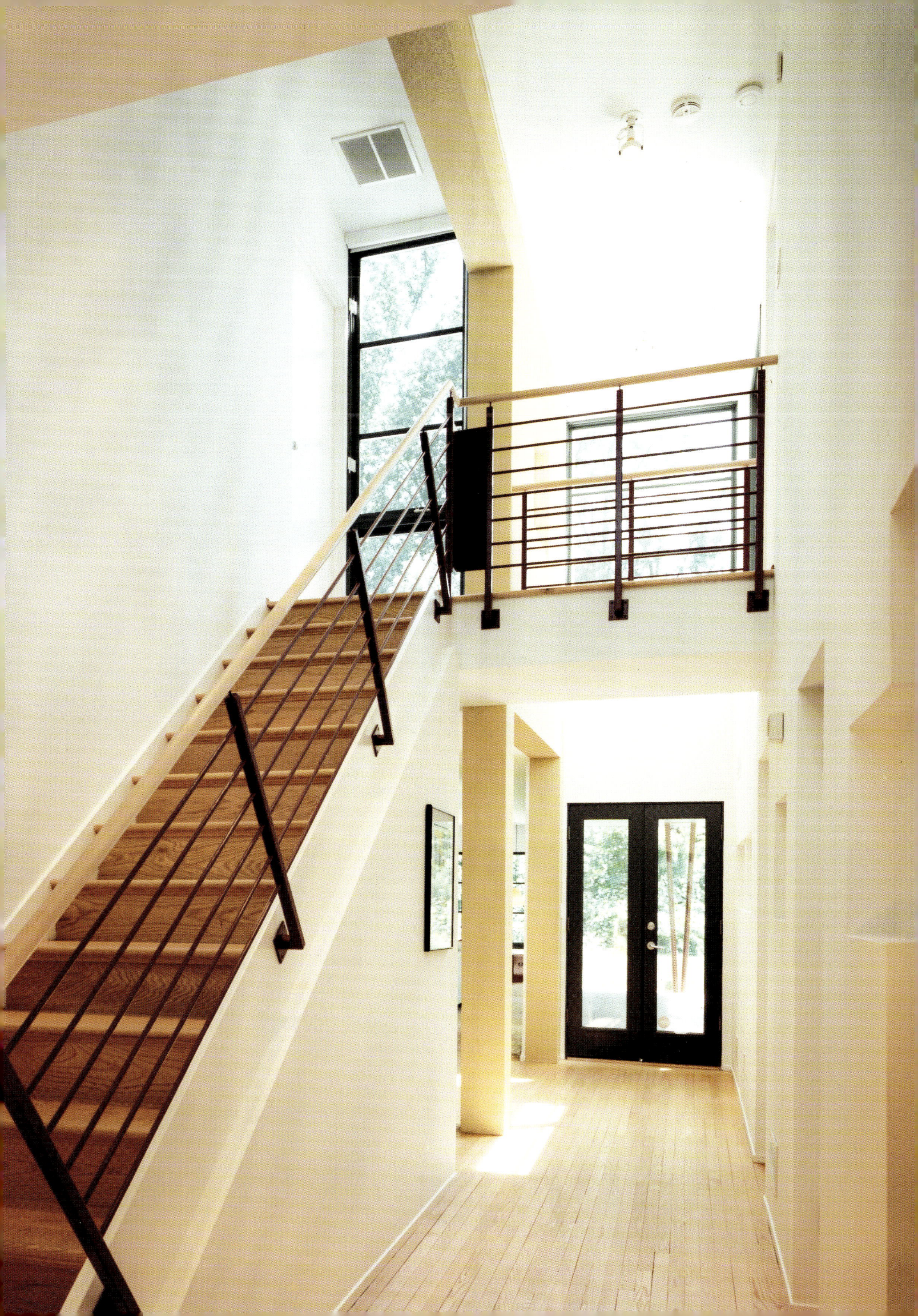

4   Street façade
5   Kitchen
6   Section perspective through stair hall
7   Axonometric

6

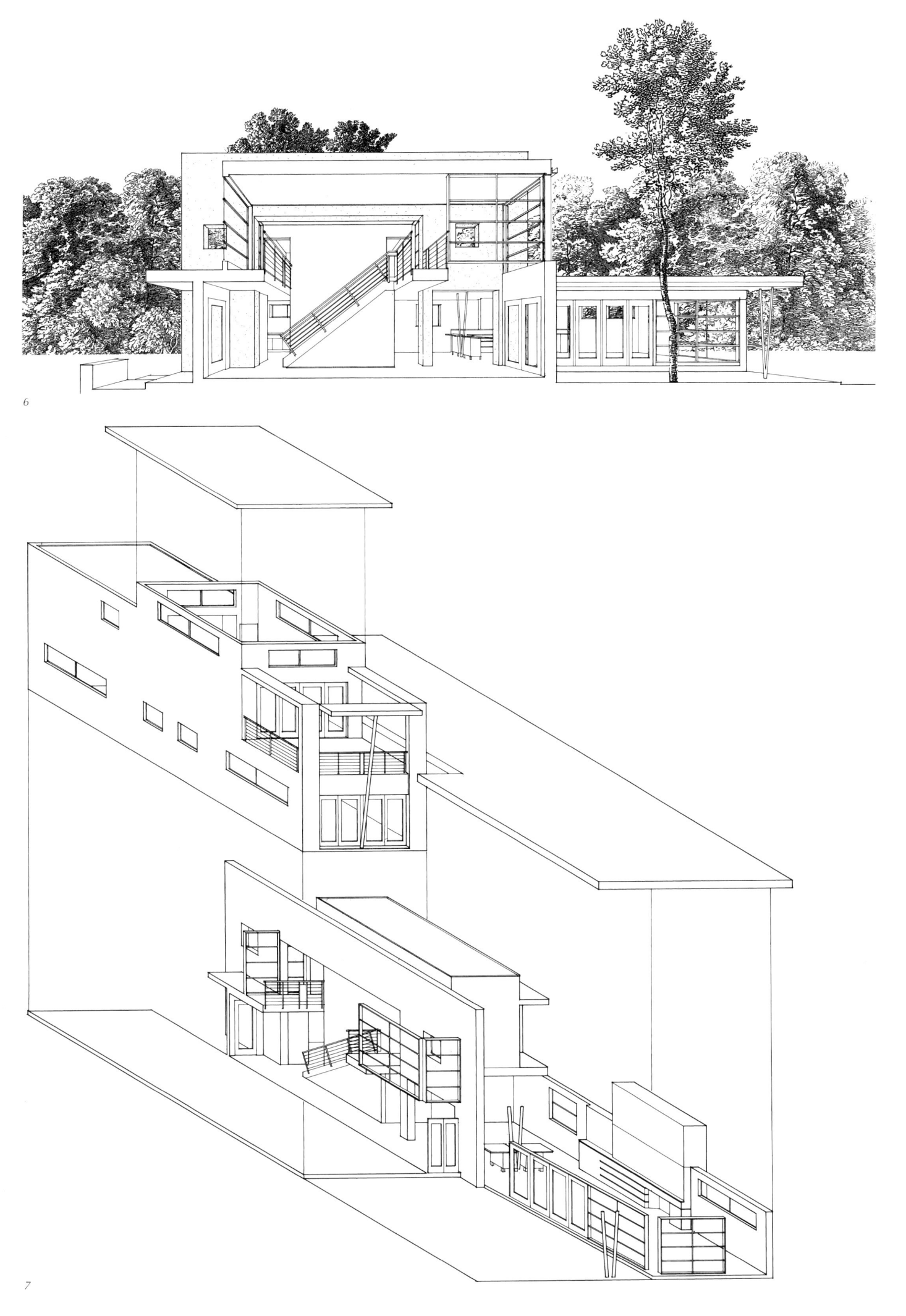

7

McInturff Architects | 49

8   Kitchen
9   Corner window in living room
10 Living room

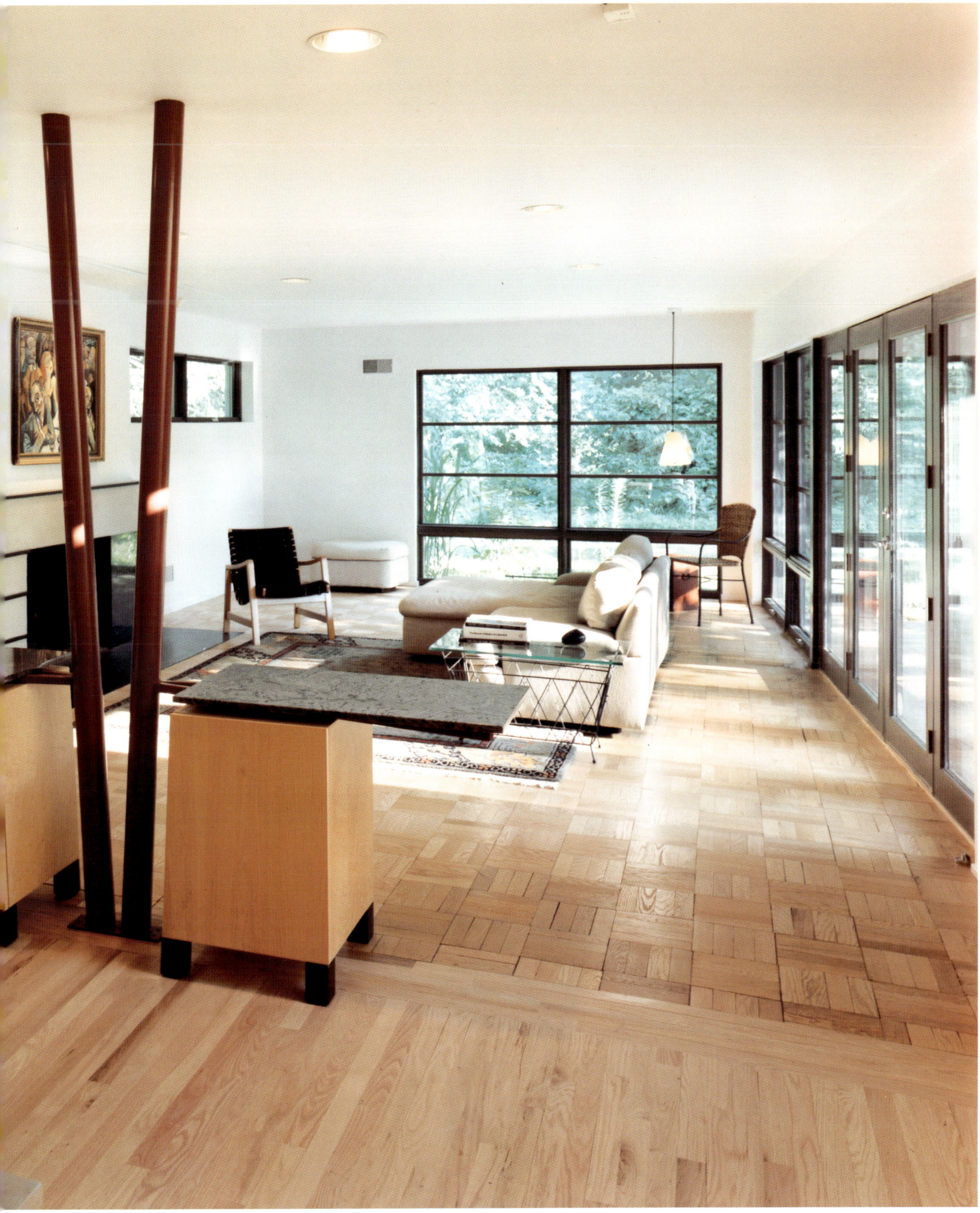

HOUSE IN THE WOODS

Bethesda, Maryland, USA
Completion: 1998

This new house occupies the site of an earlier ranch-style house that, when removed, left a linear cleared area on a site otherwise largely filled with mature trees. Designed for both private family life and large-scale entertaining, the house is organized around a lateral gallery that opens to a new terrace and the site beyond. Interior stone piers modulate this space and pick up the simple linear form of the second floor above. These piers emphasize a regular 16-foot rhythm of the elements of the building—skylights, fenestration, even downspouts—which organize both interior volumes and exterior masses.

Additional volumes—family and living rooms, screened porch, and breakfast area—project beyond the gallery and connect house to site.

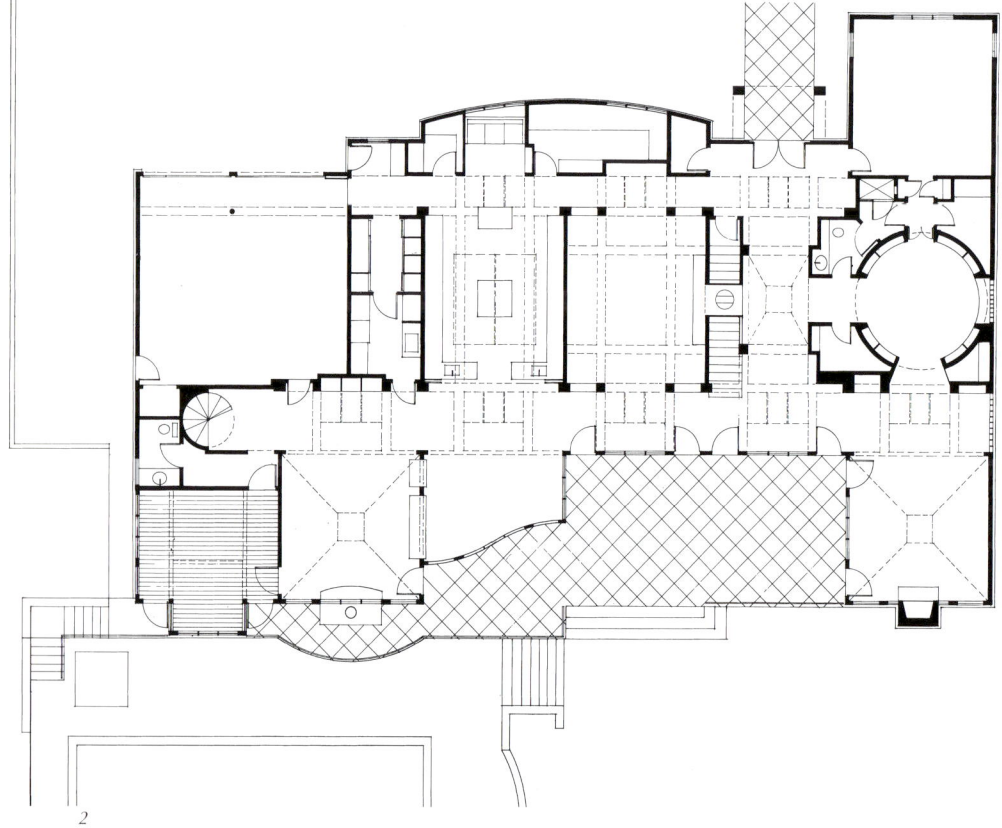

1

2

3

1   Screened porch view
2   Plan
3   Garden façade

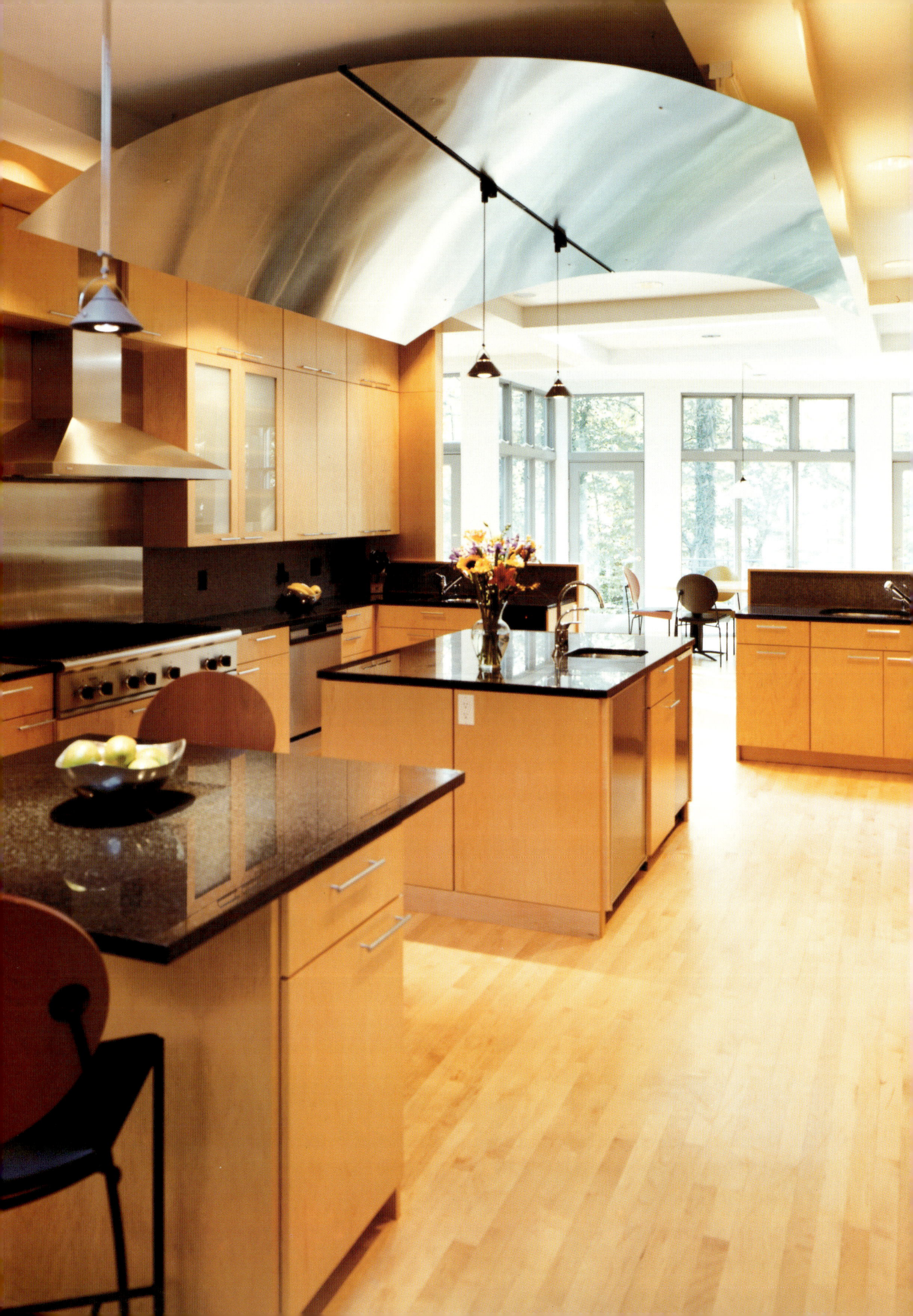

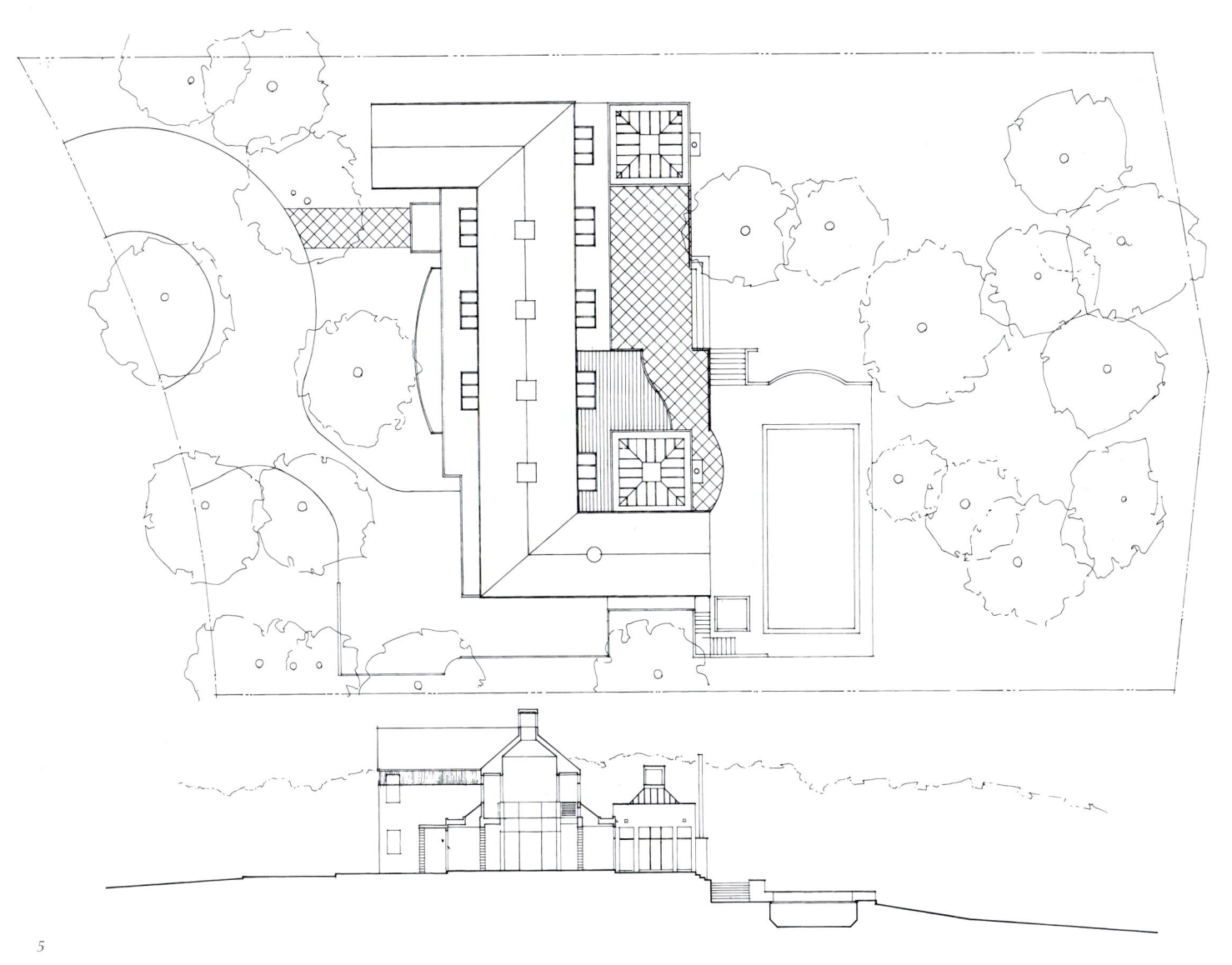

Opposite:
Kitchen
5   *Site plan and section*
6   *Breakfast room*

McInturff Architects | 55

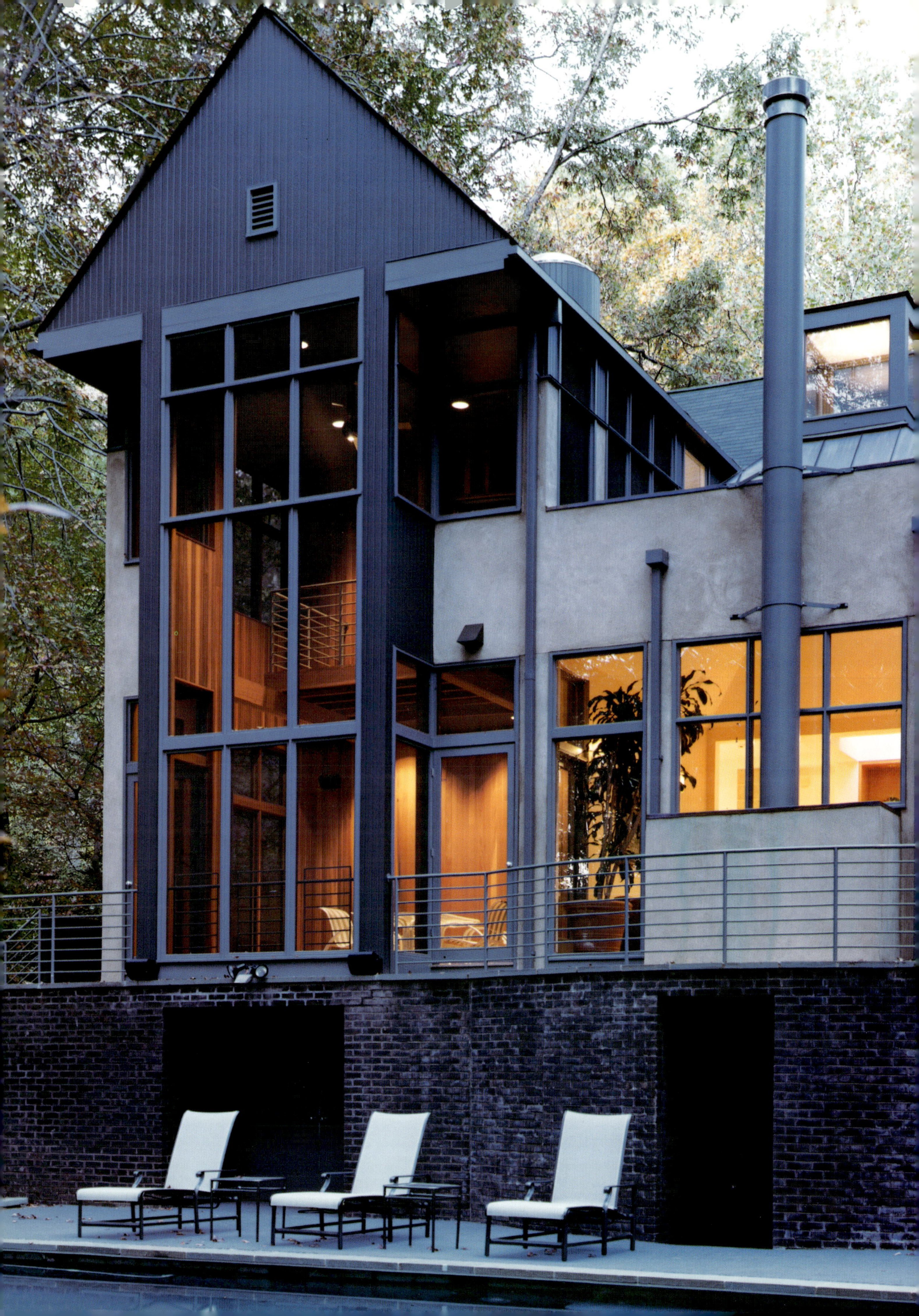

Opposite:
  Porch and pool view
8 *Gallery view*
9 *Library; carpet design by architect*

HEARD TENG RESIDENCE II

Washington DC, USA
Completion: 1998

1   *Garden plan*
2   *Lower lawn with pool beyond*
Opposite:
   Library at night from terrace

The owners of a pre-war, center hall house that we had remodeled to a more modern style in the late 1980s, came to us with the request for a new garden design. Requirements included the addition of a swimming pool, the reduction of grass/lawn area, redesign of an existing wood pergola, and in general, a more gracious connection between the existing house and its large but largely disconnected and under-used yard.

Placing the new swimming pool at the rear of the property takes advantage of the extraordinary depth of the lot, creating a destination that, with the sequence of spaces leading to it, activates the entire yard. The new library, seen as a garden room, sits on a stone wall which continues out into the garden to define a perfect rectangle of grass. The excavation that created the lawn allows the main level of the house to connect deep into the garden; previously, one walked only three steps out the door before confronting a retaining wall. A pavilion at the corner of the house, opposite the library, mirrors the library in plan, and provides a shady location for exterior dining and seating.

Additional structures—a pergola, stairs, spiral terrace, and pool pavilions for seating and to house pool equipment—loosely mark the boundaries of the garden. The original pergola was replaced, continuing the rhythm of the concrete columns of the library out into the garden.

A limited palette of materials—stone walls, sandblasted concrete columns, bluestone and limestone paving, and fir—were used in various combinations throughout the garden. These materials were carried into the interior of the library, where a wood plank bridge creates a threshold in a space made luminous by panels of sandblasted glass, supporting the illusion of leaving the house and moving into an exterior room. The stone step and patterned stone floor further connect the library to the architecture of the garden.

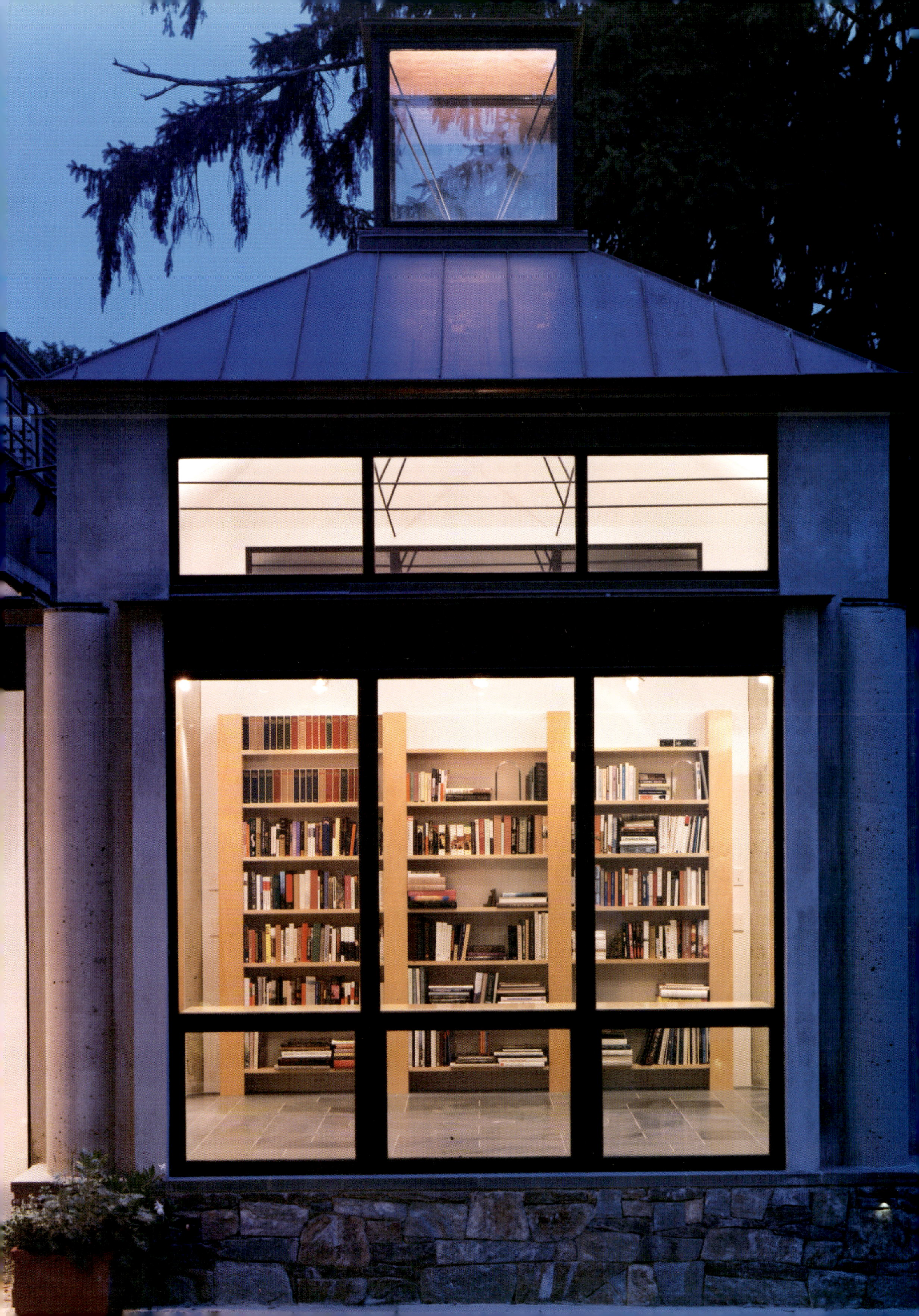

4 Detail of entry to library
5 Garden structures
6 Library from family room

McInturff Architects | *61*

7

8
9
10

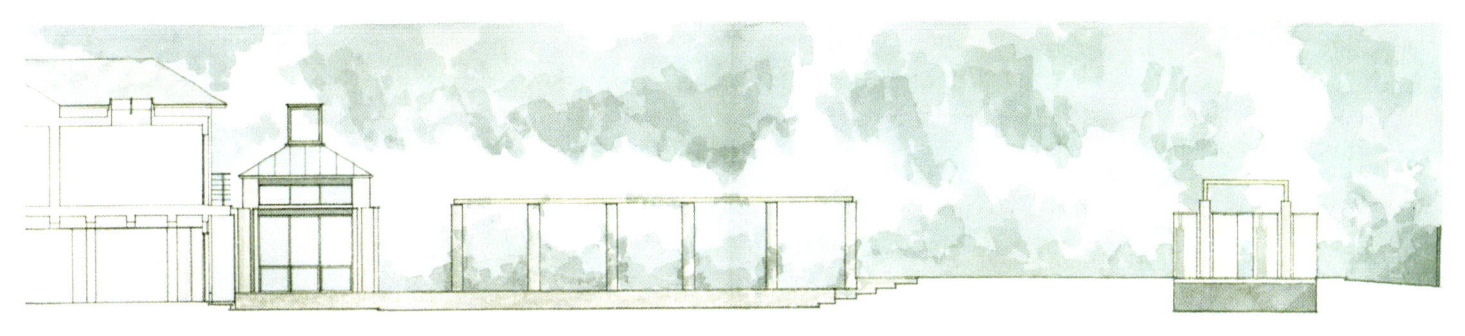

7 Library
8,9&10 Sections and elevations
11 Library cupola and tie rods

11

McInturff Architects | 63

ARMSTRONG HOUSE

Merry-Go-Round Farms, Potomac, Maryland, USA
Completion: 1999

1 View from woods
2 Entry façade
3 Section through bridge, entry and living room

This house, designed for a couple with two grown children, attempts to simplify the lives of the owners by providing a small number of generous spaces in lieu of a larger number of particularized rooms. Requisite bedrooms include one on the main level for future accessibility needs; the program is otherwise reduced to an intimately scaled library, a generous, open kitchen, and a large double-height room for living and dining. This room takes the form of a half cylinder, gathering in the views of the wooded site, while the remainder of the house fits within an orderly bar. A skylit slot separates these two pieces. A landing at the top of the stairs occupies this slot and all circulation within the house involves moving between the two pieces. Materials—concrete, steel, glass, and wood—have been used in ways that express their natural properties.

McInturff Architects | 65

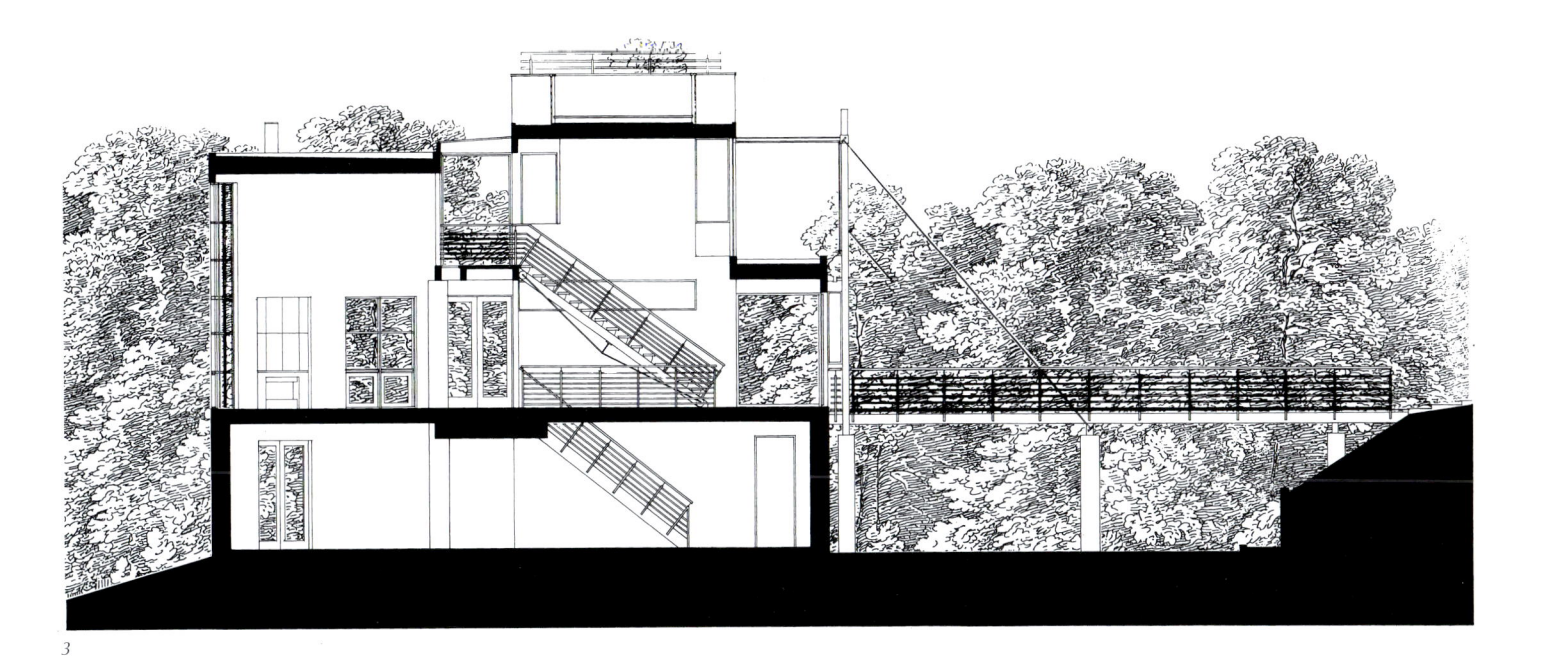

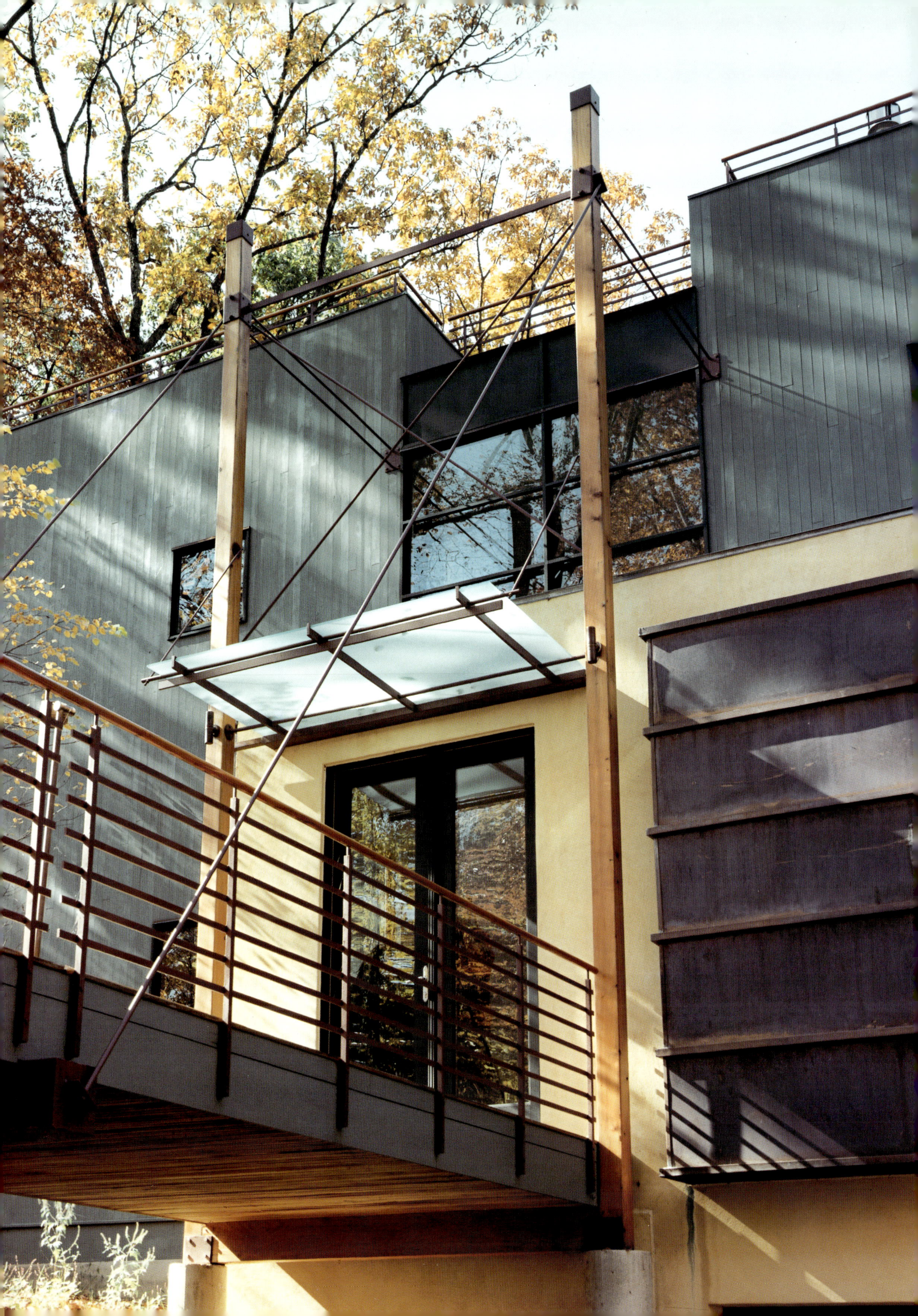

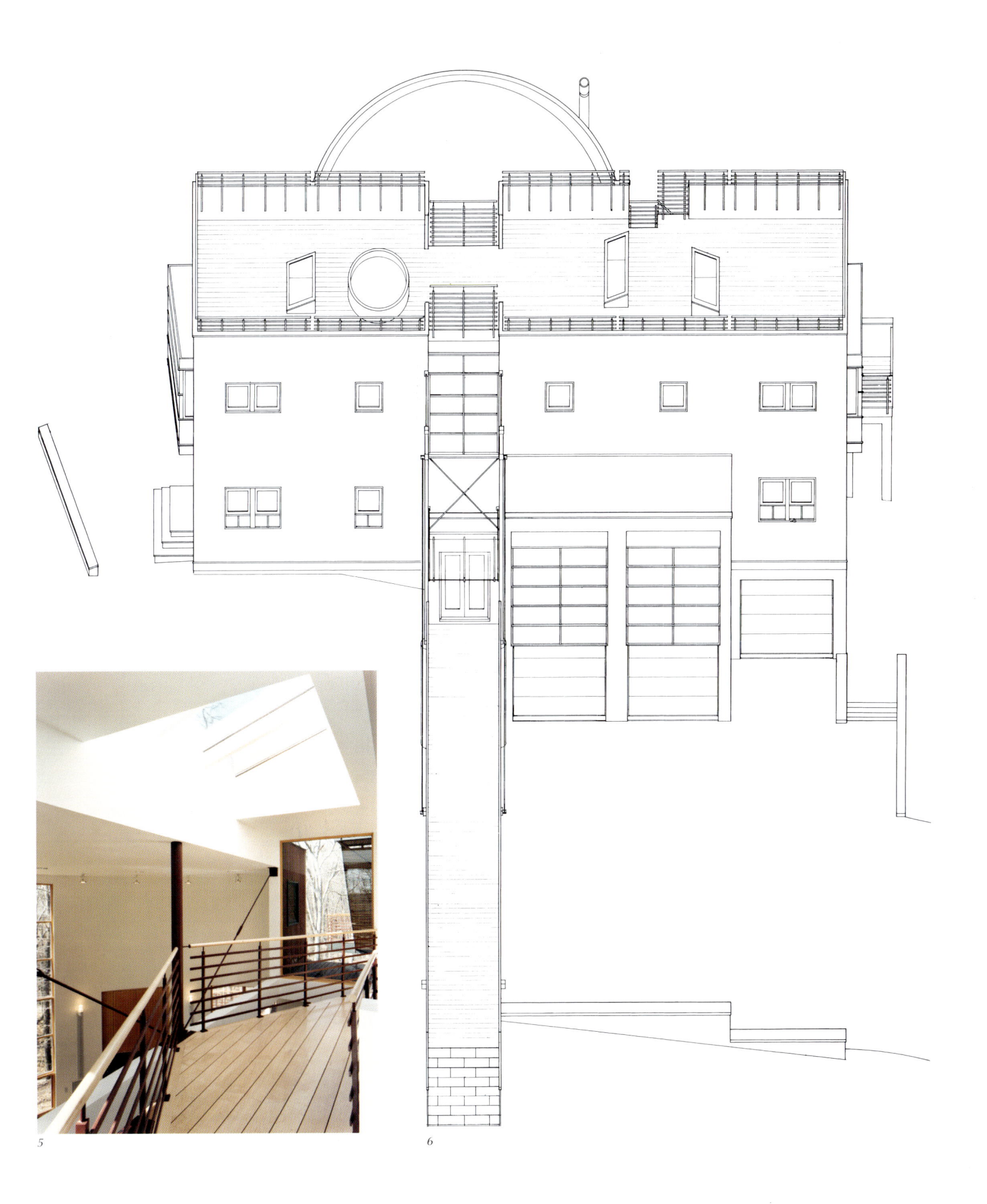

Opposite:
 Entry bridge detail
5 Stair landing
6 Axonometric, entry side

McInturff Architects | 67

7   Plans
8   Entry bridge model
Opposite:
    Detail of column, stair, and landing

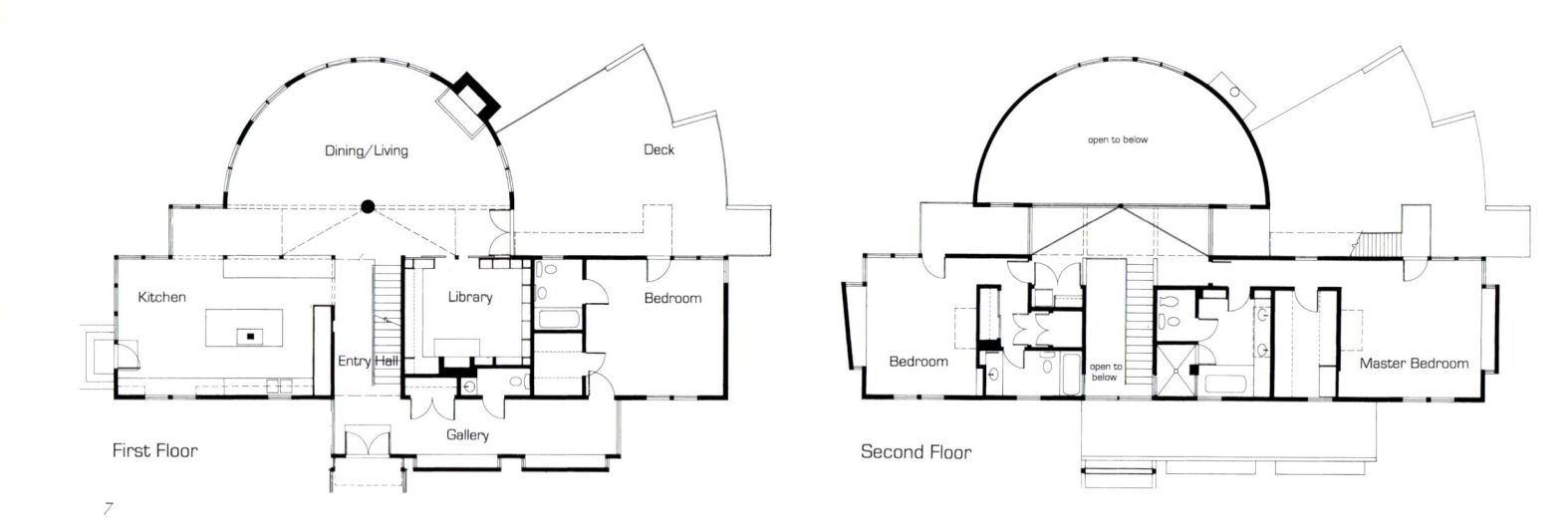

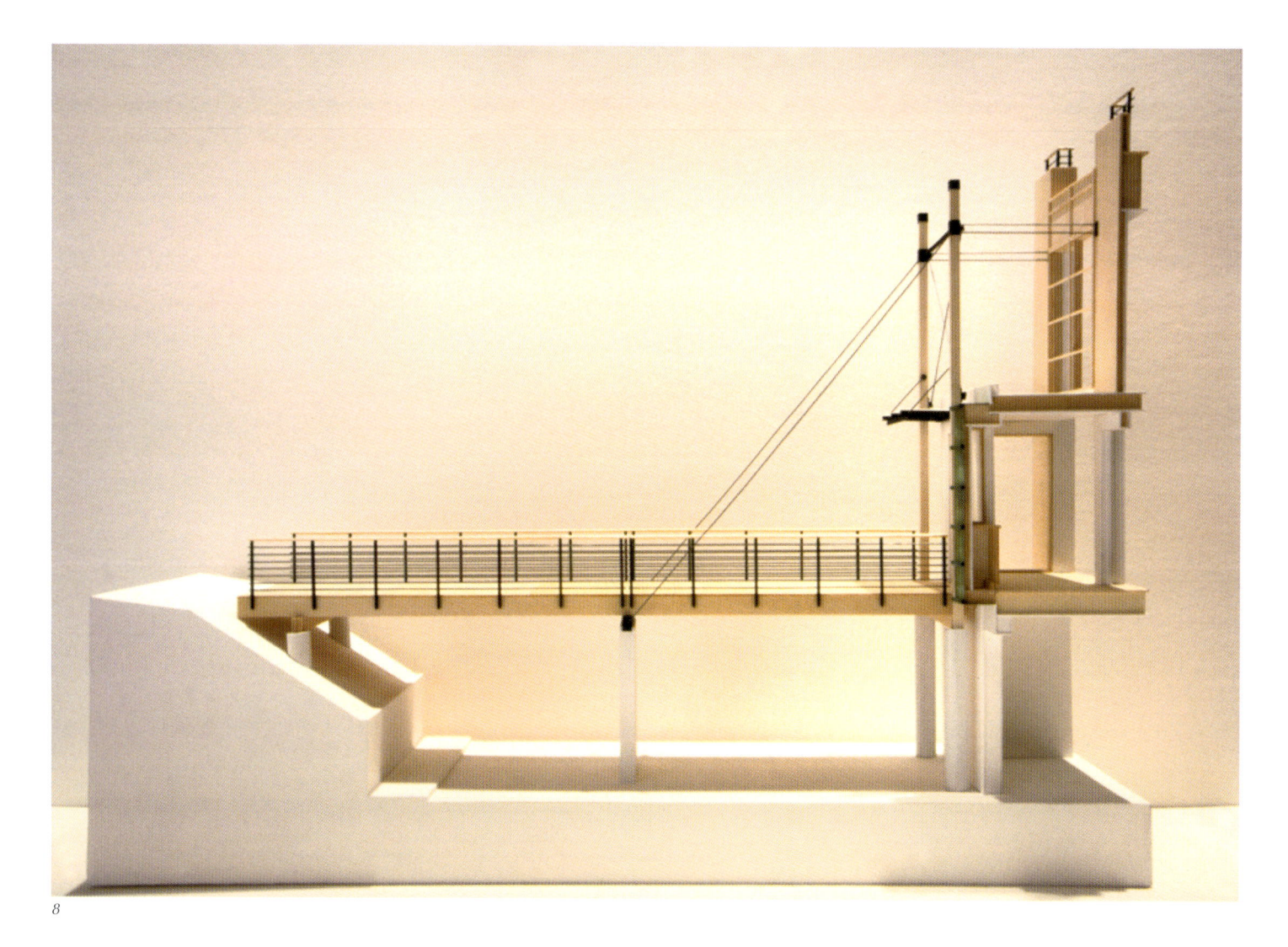

First Floor

Second Floor

7

8

68 | ARMSTRONG HOUSE

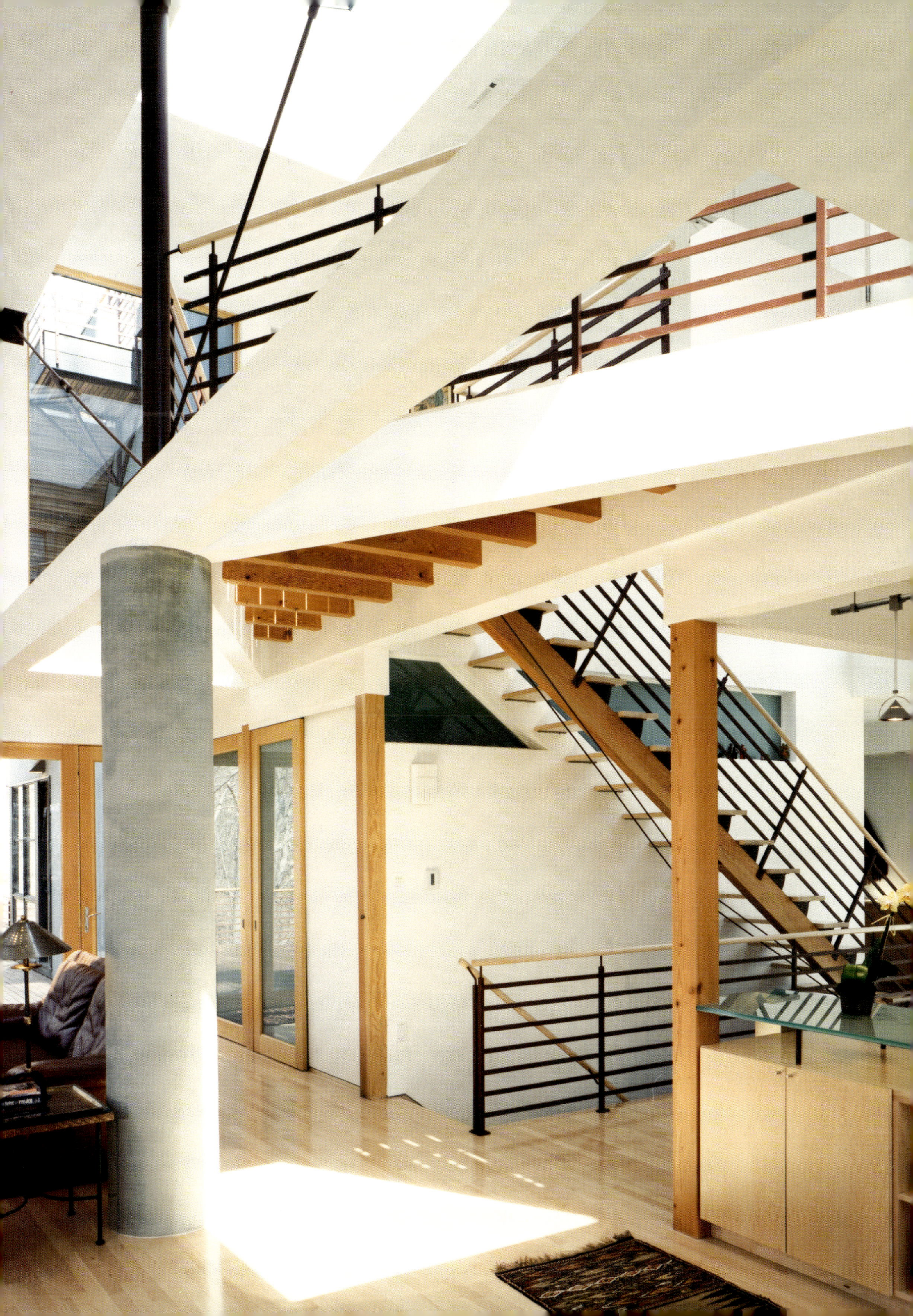

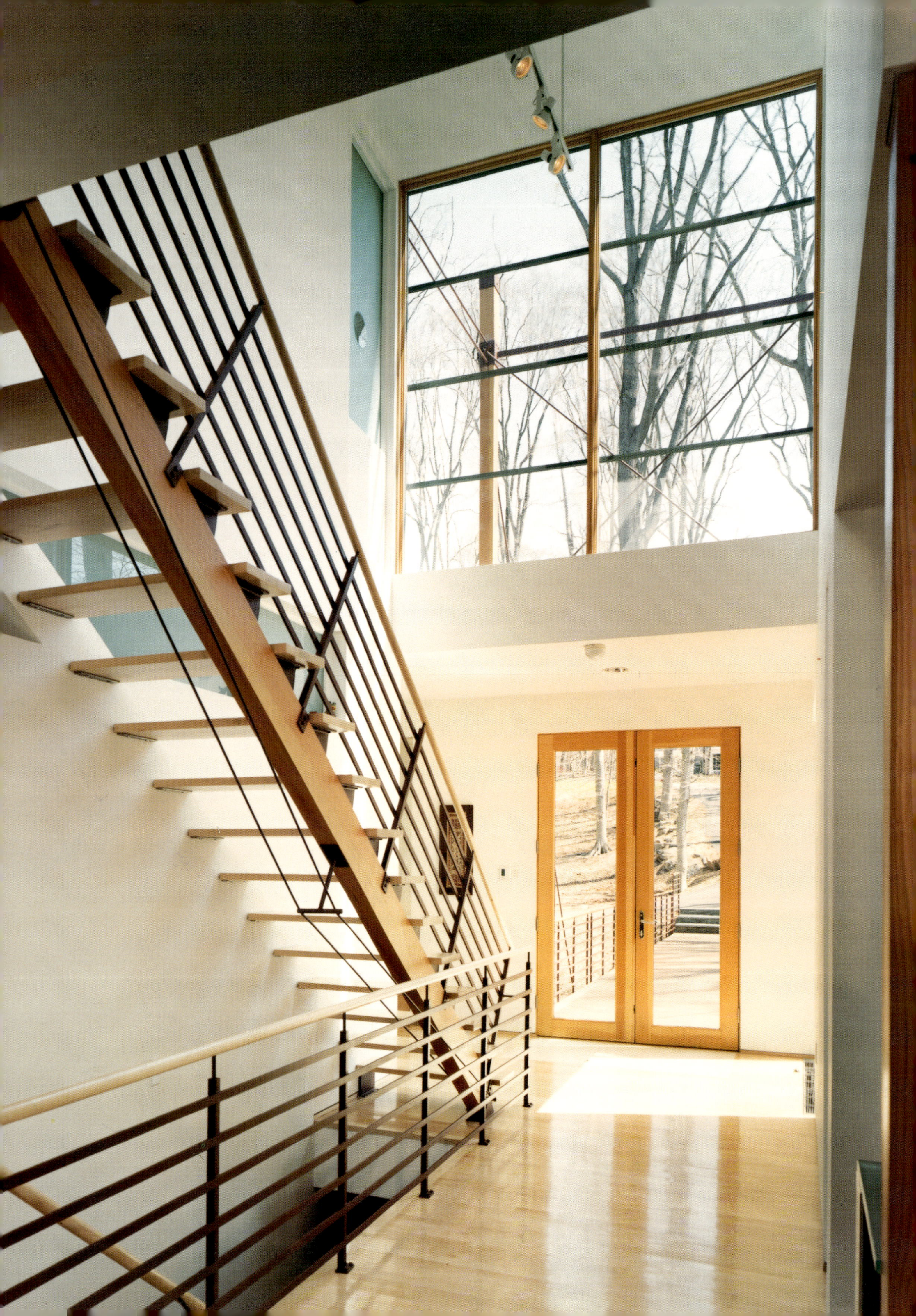

Opposite:
    Entry hall
11 Side view with woods beyond
12 Gallery
13 Living room
14 View from kitchen with living room beyond

McInturff Architects | 71

RESIDENCE IN OLD TOWN

Alexandria, Virginia, USA
Completion: 1999

1   Axonometric
Opposite:
   Kitchen

This project involved the rejuvenation of the connective tissue of a small collection of historic buildings in Alexandria, Virginia. Over time, a suite of rooms had infilled areas between a Second Empire town house, a service building (or 'flounder,' as they are locally known), and a garage. A previous renovation of these spaces had created a strange, amorphous kitchen and family room suite. The acquisition of a small neighboring house gave the property a new guesthouse with a shared garden between, and allowed for a reorganization. A new breakfast room now projects into the shared garden; the kitchen—formerly with a 7-foot ceiling—has been reconfigured in the now double-height 'flounder' space. The family room is enlarged, and the circulation clarified. Throughout, materials were chosen for their expressive potential, with the intent that the connective spaces within this historic ensemble have an identity of their own.

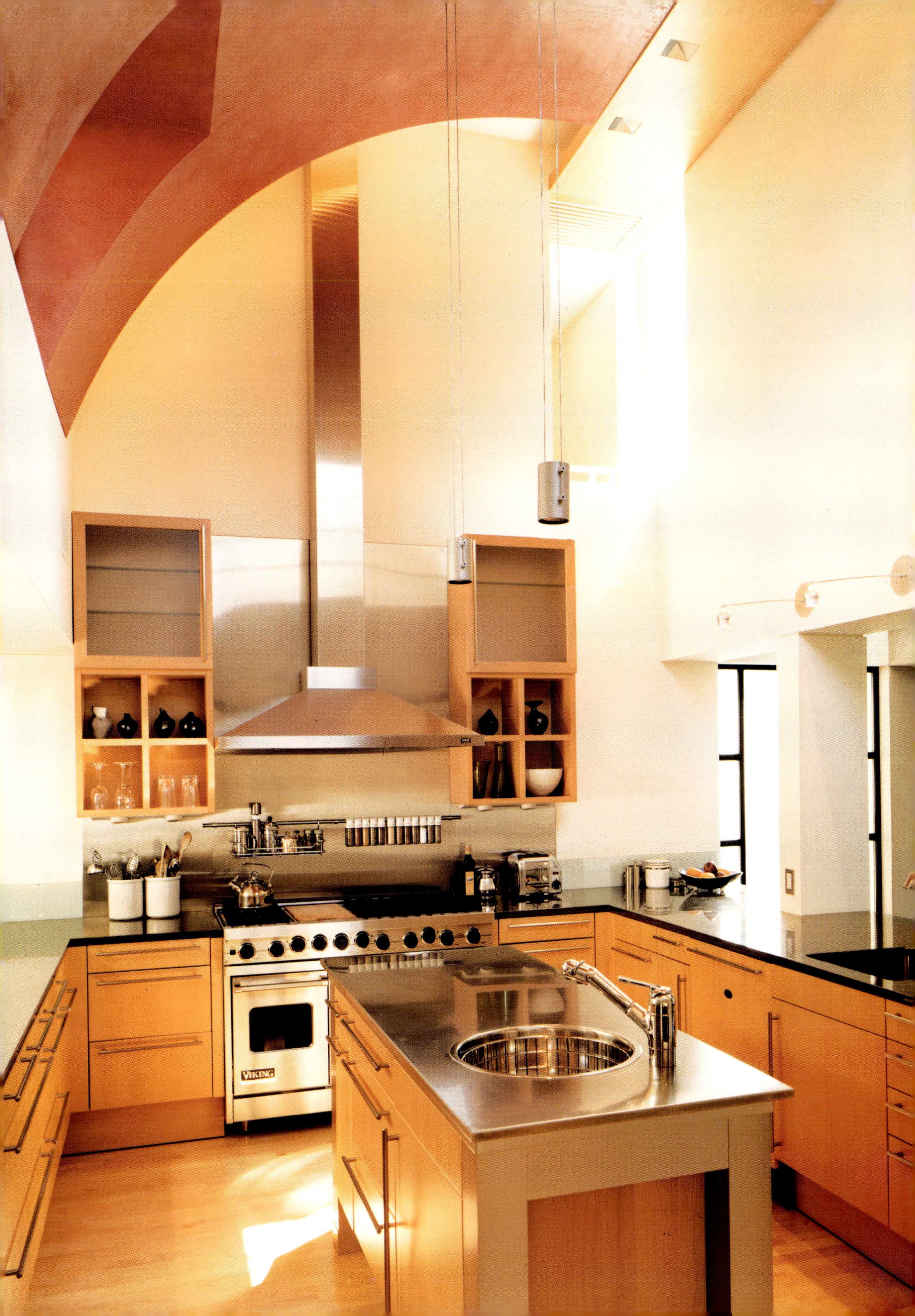
VIKING

3

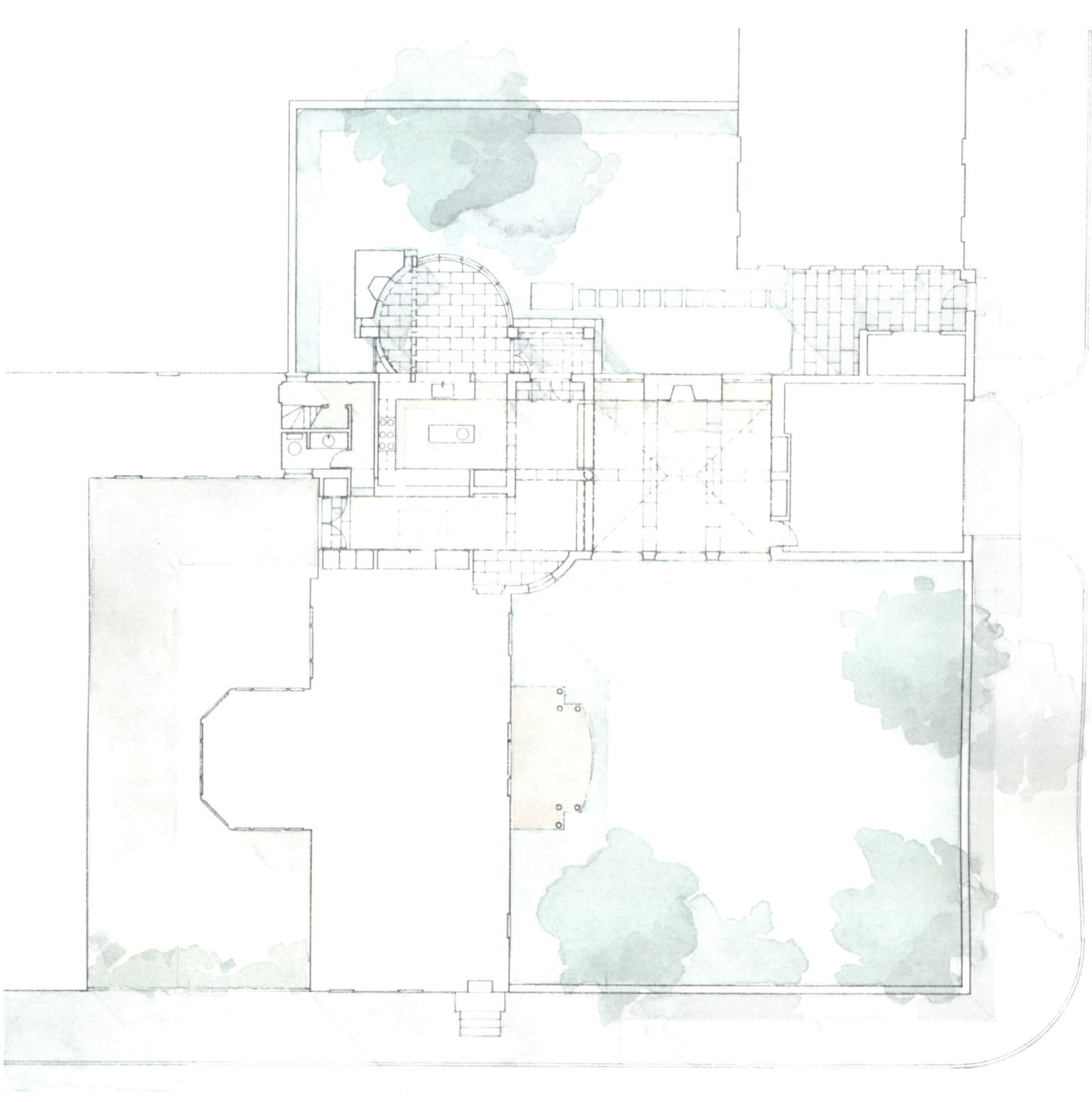

4

74 | RESIDENCE IN OLD TOWN

3   Garden view
4   Plan, after
5   Family room

6   Detail of breakfast room
7   Night view of breakfast room
Opposite:
    Kitchen

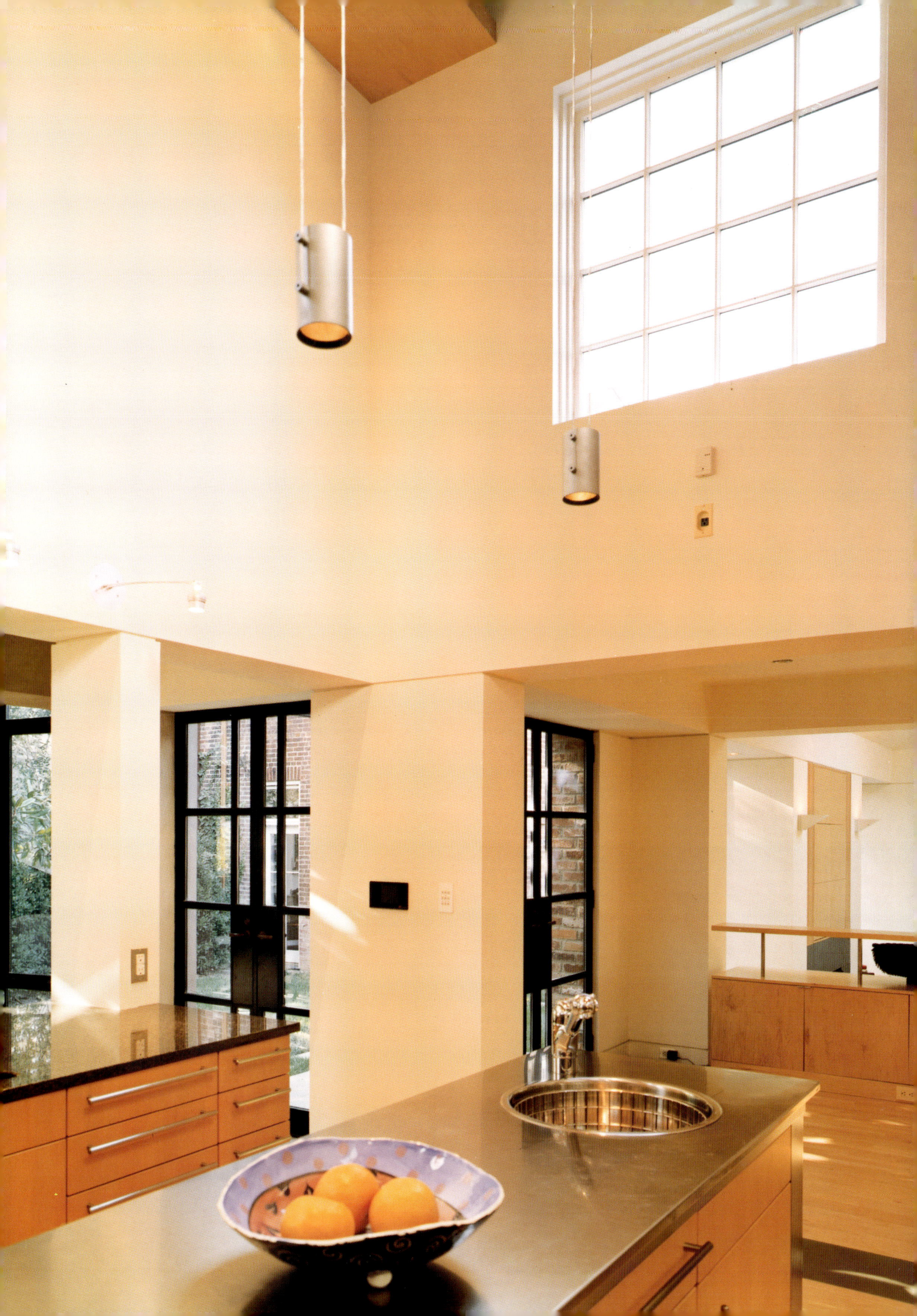

9 Breakfast room
10 Breakfast room in garden
11 Plan, before
12 Kitchen

10

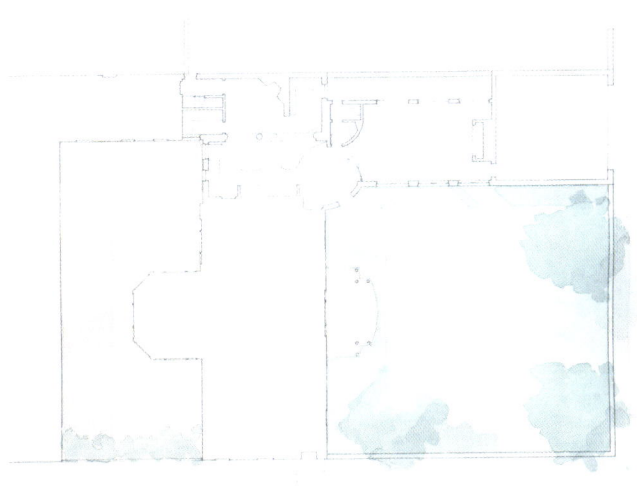

11

12

McInturff Architects | 79

HANSON SCIANNELLA RESIDENCE

Rockville, Maryland, USA
Completion: 1999

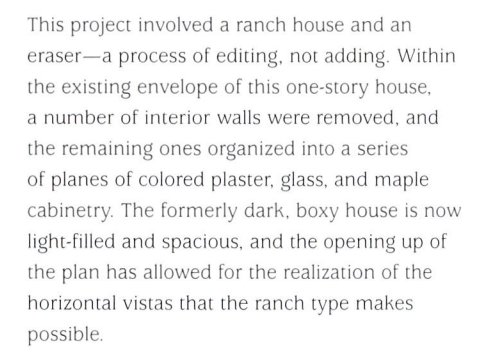

2

This project involved a ranch house and an eraser—a process of editing, not adding. Within the existing envelope of this one-story house, a number of interior walls were removed, and the remaining ones organized into a series of planes of colored plaster, glass, and maple cabinetry. The formerly dark, boxy house is now light-filled and spacious, and the opening up of the plan has allowed for the realization of the horizontal vistas that the ranch type makes possible.

1 Detail of view toward entry
2 Dining room
Opposite:
   View from kitchen

1

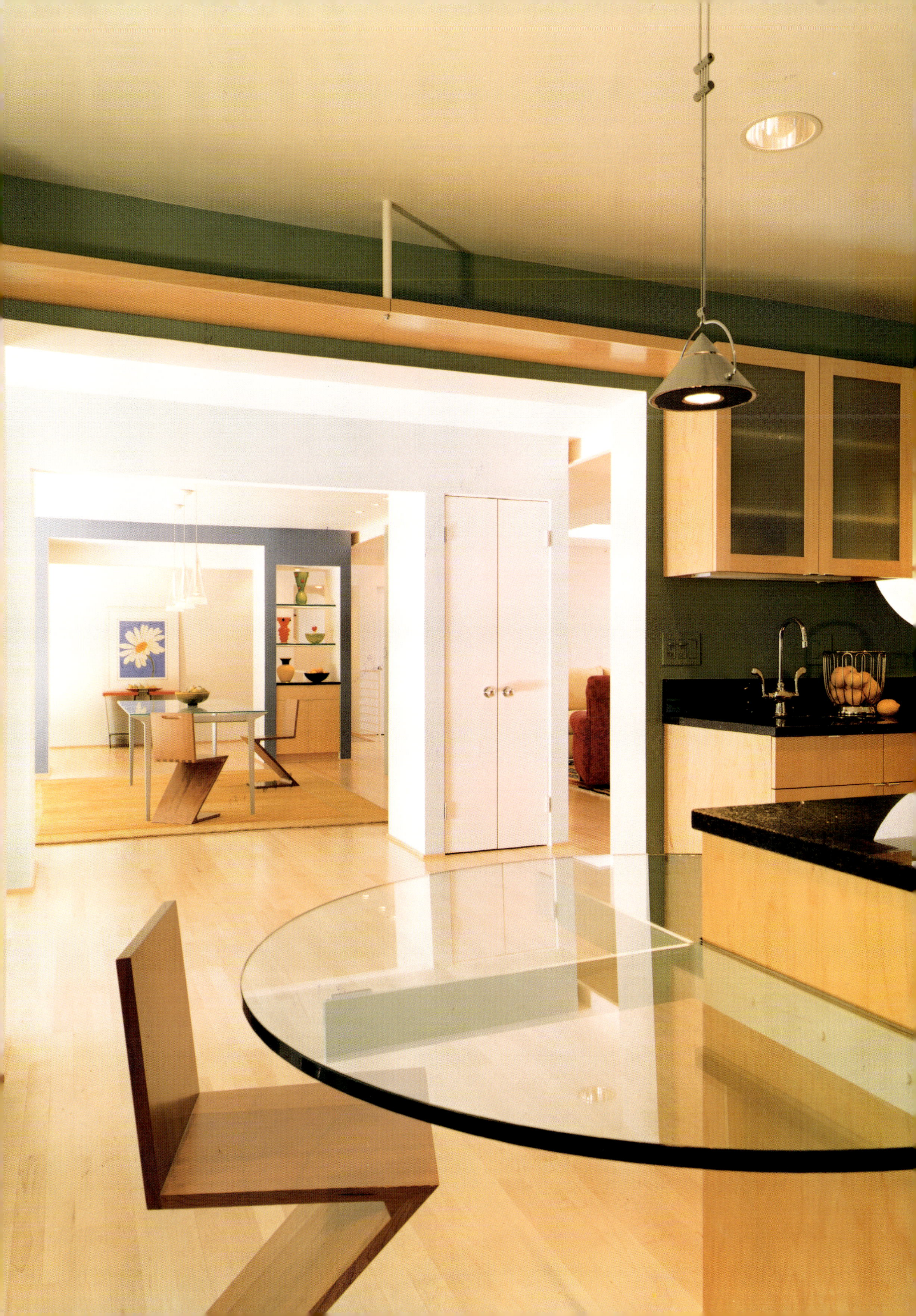

4

5

6

82 | HANSON SCIANNELLA RESIDENCE

4   Axonometric
5   Living room
6   Dining room

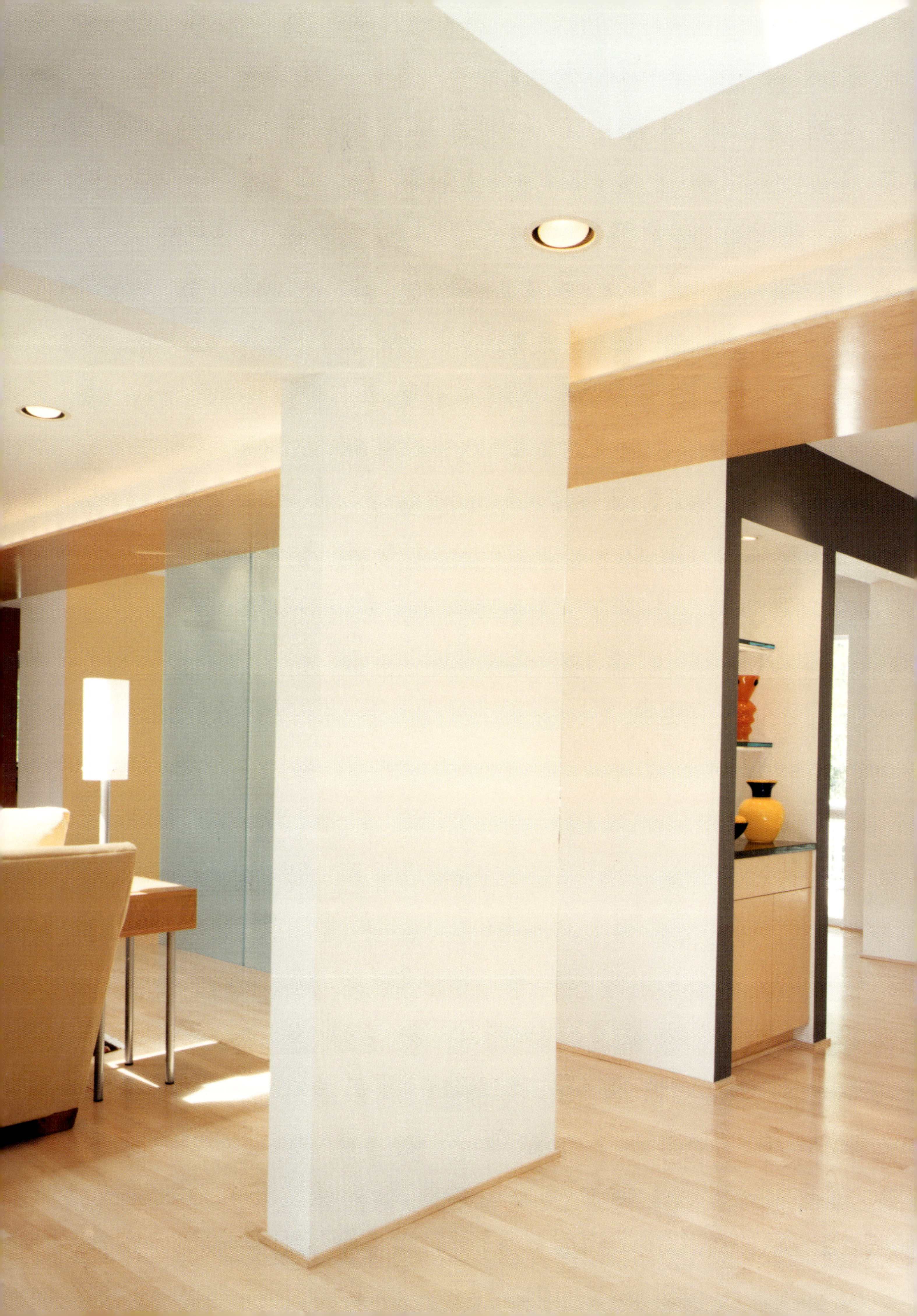

Opposite:

8   Plans, before and after
9   Glass wall with dining room beyond

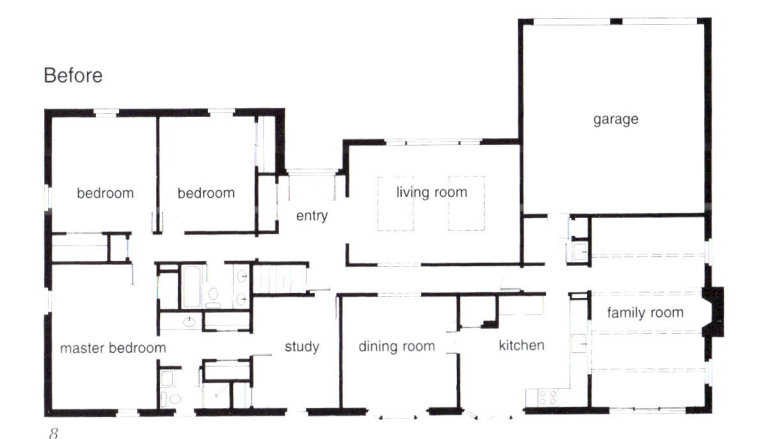

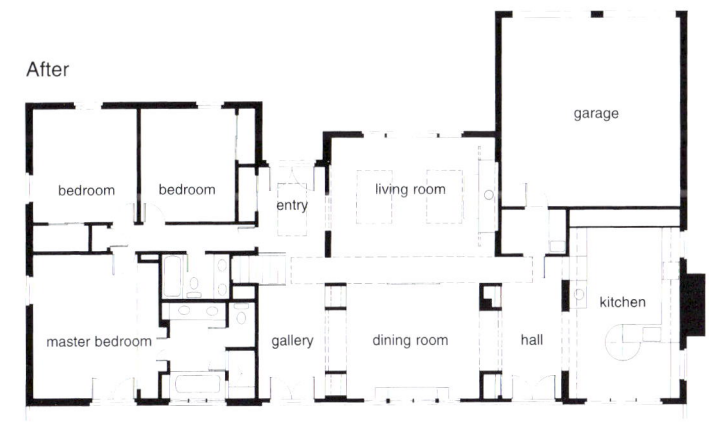

Before

After

WEINER RESIDENCE II

Washington DC, USA
Completion: 1999

1 Section
2 New garden façade

Historically, the block structure of Washington allowed, and even encouraged, an outer row of middle-class townhouses on the street, and an inner row of small working-class houses on a mid-block alley or court. A handful of courts survive on Capitol Hill, and one provides the site for this project. Our client had lived here for a decade when he got the chance to buy the tiny adjacent house, and, more compelling, its even tinier garden. The client's existing house occupied its entire 14-foot by 44-foot lot, with no outdoor space. The owner had no specific new functional requirements, so the acquired space could be seen as a variety of stages and places from which to revel in all 200 square feet of the new garden.

The added house—11 feet wide, 30 feet long and two stories high—was gutted. Party walls were stripped to the brick and painted white, and the back wall was carved away to provide a new window-wall connecting inside and out. New openings in the former party wall now connect the two buildings. Within the bright, open volume of the new space, a stepped wooden platform has been suspended, providing seating adjacent to the original second floor living room.

Beneath this platform is a space that serves as a new master bedroom. Next to this, and overlooked by the platform, is a double-height volume that becomes a sort of interior courtyard for the now joined buildings, providing access from each to the garden. A balcony from the original second floor living area overlooks this space. Fir louvers shade the interior and provide some privacy from nearby neighbors.

Conventional ideas of room types and adjacencies were of little concern; more interesting to all involved was the making of spaces ranging from intimate to theatrical, animating house and site, and extracting from the small added square footage far more benefit than it had ever provided as a separate house.

1

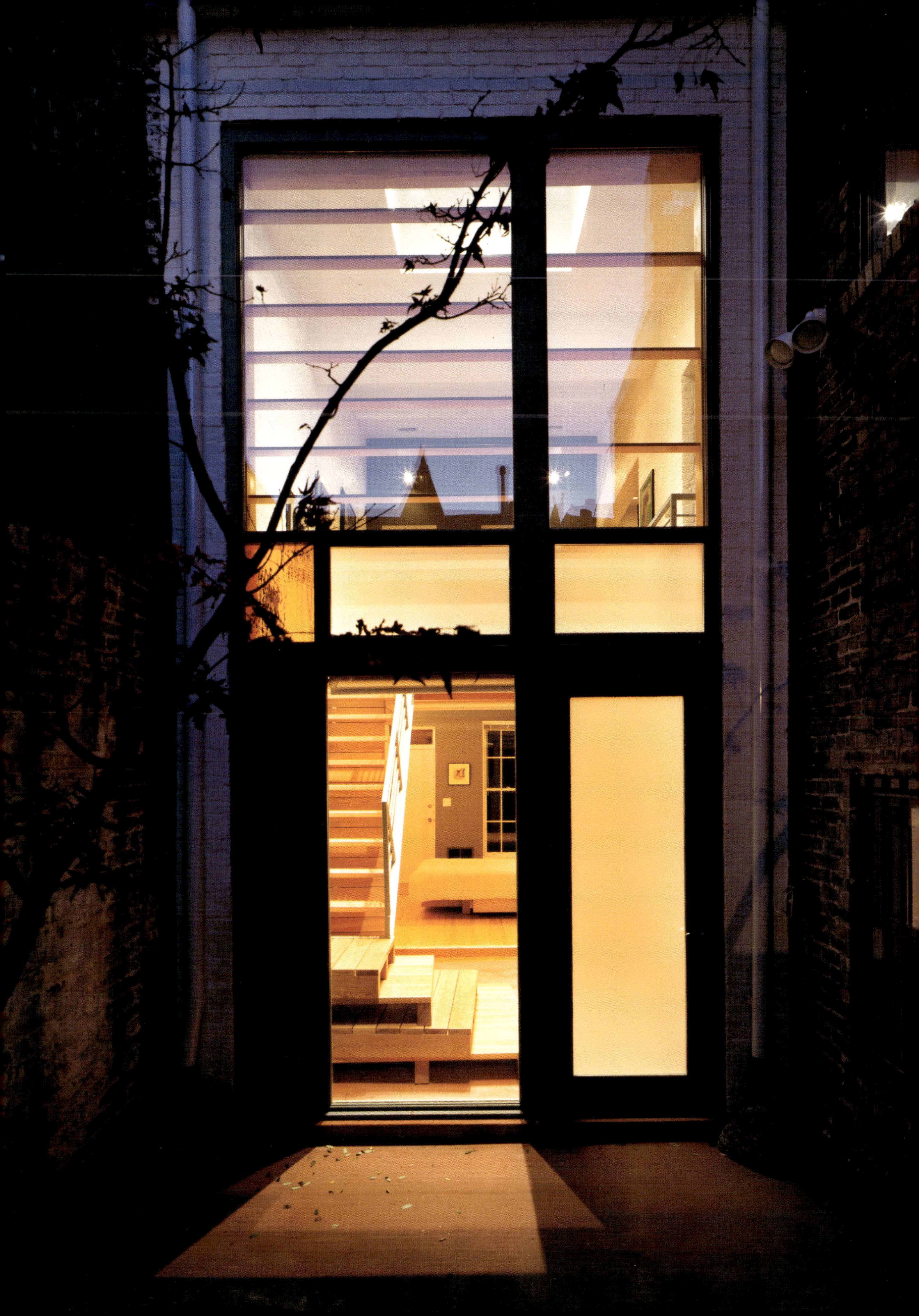

3

3 View of seating platforms above new bedroom
4 Model
5 Plans, after
6 Bed detail

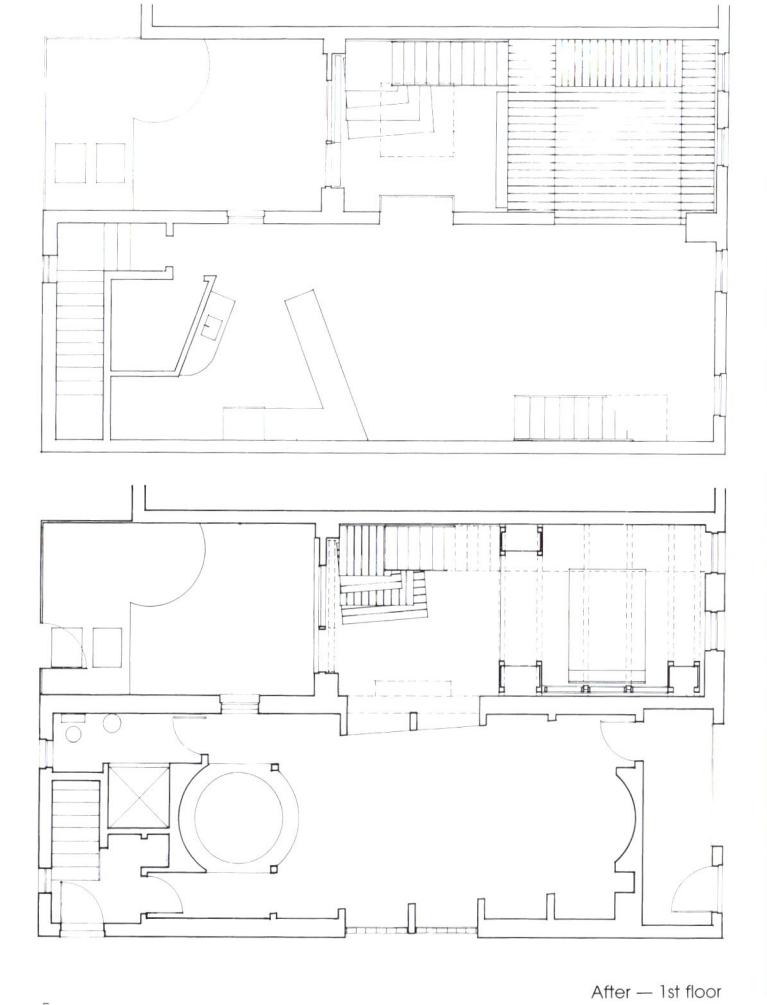

After — 2nd floor

After — 1st floor

McInturff Architects | 89

7 Stair detail
8 Seating platforms
9 Bed detail
10 Stair to seating platforms viewed from new kitchen balcony

Opposite:
  View from bedroom

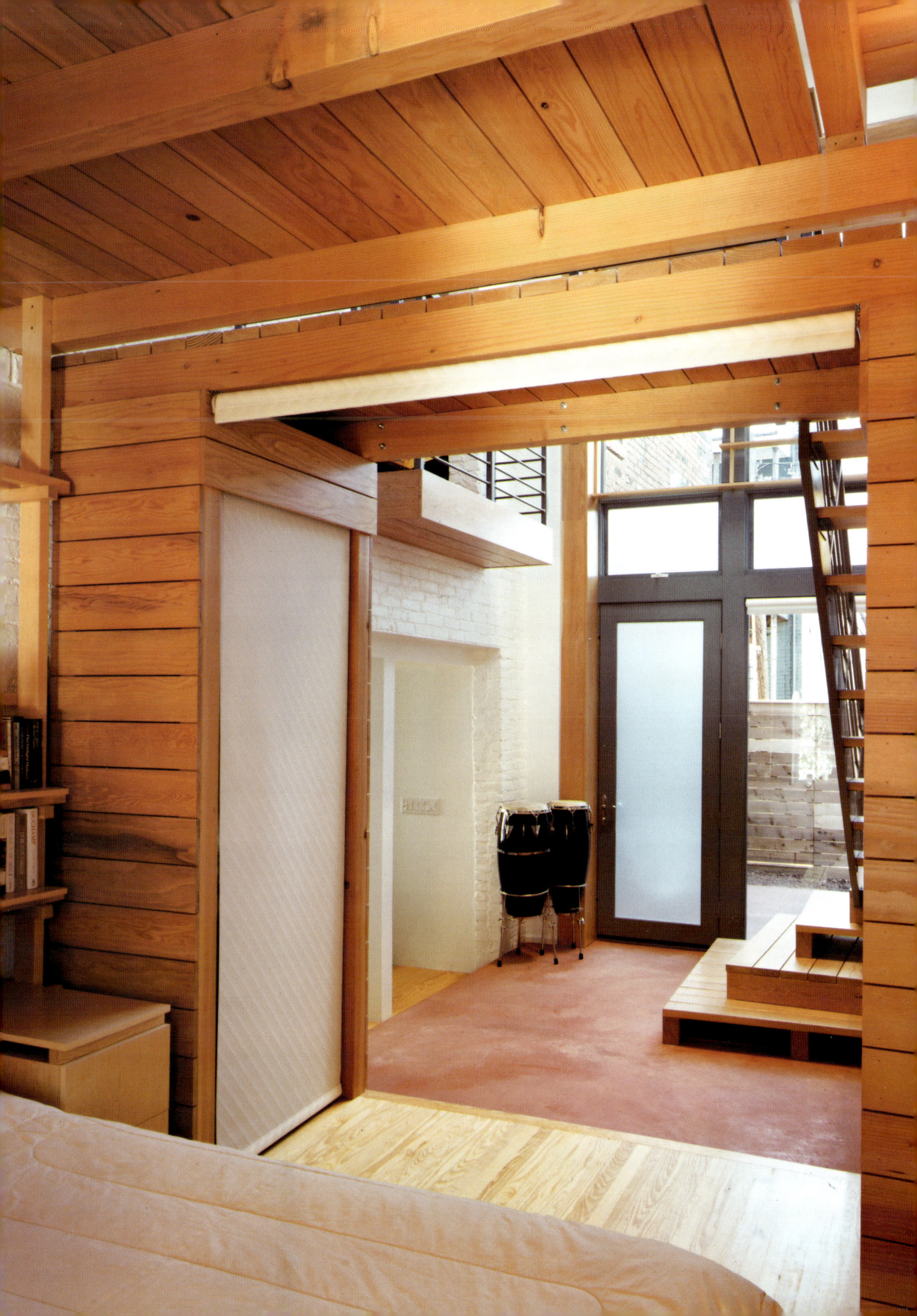

WITHERS HOUSE

Accokeek, Maryland, USA
Completion: 1998

This tiny house, designed for a professor of art history, occupies a wooded 10-acre site in rural Maryland. The client, who grew up in New England in a house designed by Dan Kiley, asked for two things: a simple and inexpensive cabin in the woods in the spirit of the Kiley house, and the proper setting for a commissioned artwork, a sun drawing by artist Janet Saad Cook.

The cabin exists in the two asphalt-shingled, tightly functional wings. Saad Cook is in the middle, in a metal and glass room that bridges the wings. This space, which houses the living and dining areas, is designed around this piece. Here, the sun drawing projects reflected images, which change with the movement of the sun and clouds, onto a wall—an ephemeral response to place, time and architecture. The glass wall is to the north, and the second-story bridge that connects the two wings runs in front of it. This allows the south wall to receive the projected image on a billboard-like surface, which itself allows south light in only at the floor and ceiling.

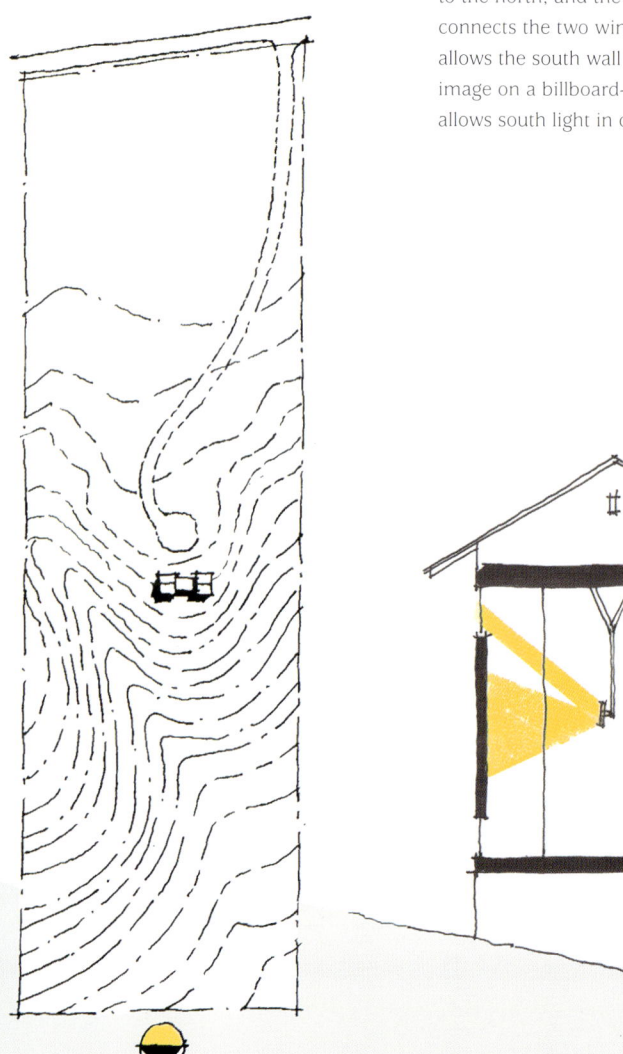

1   Site plan and section detail showing sun drawing
    armature
2   View of north wall from downhill, showing bridge
    structure

McInturff Architects | 93

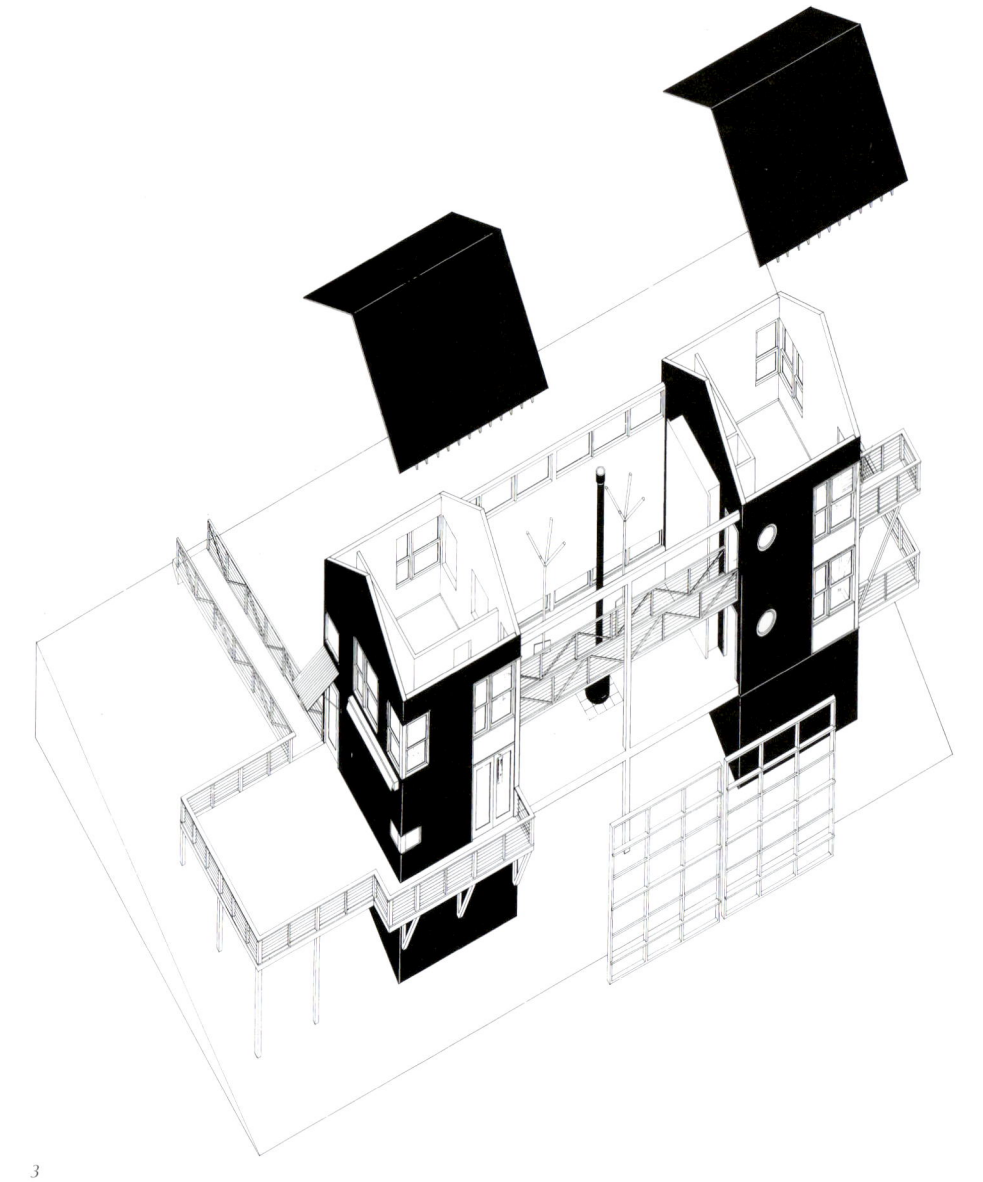

3   Axonometric
4   Model
Opposite:
   View of great room showing interior bridge and glass wall; sliding corrugated metal panels cover study windows

94 | WITHERS HOUSE

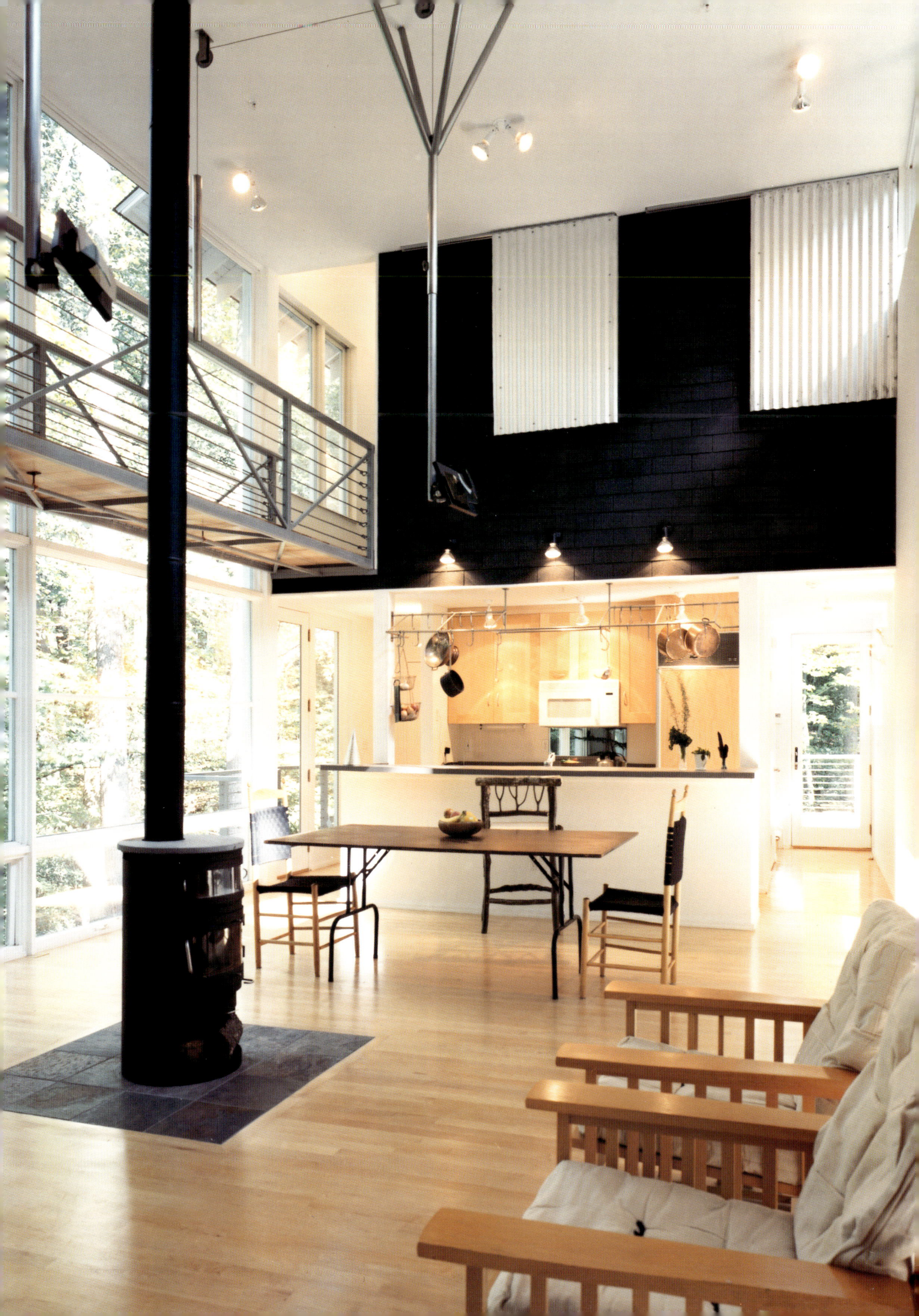

6 View of west tower
7 Entry view with billboard-like wall for sun drawings
8 View of south wall
9 View of great room with counterweighted armatures that allow seasonal adjustments to sun drawings

96 | WITHERS HOUSE

8

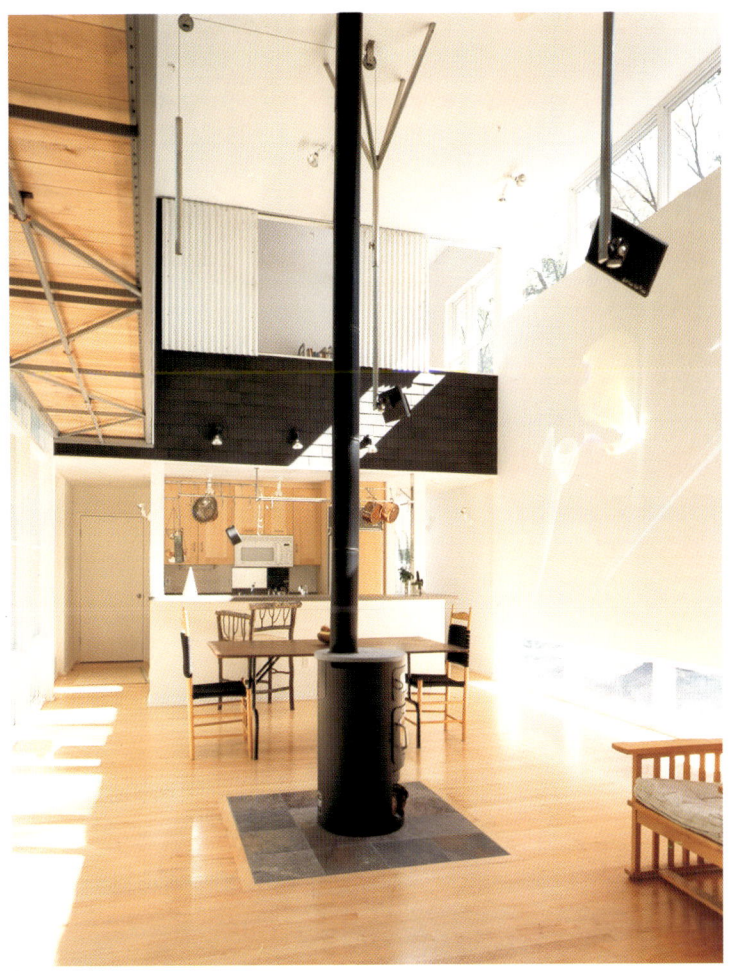

9

COZZENS RESIDENCE

Washington DC, USA
Completion: 2000

1 Potomac River elevation at night
2 Potomac River elevation
Opposite:
 Teak sunscreens on river elevation

When our client bought this prominently sited Georgetown house he thought it needed new bathrooms. Subsequent inspection revealed that the back of the house, having been built on 60 feet of fill, was migrating south.

New helical steel piers, some more than 60 feet long, have stabilized the movement of the structure, and a new steel frame gives rigidity to the four-story back addition that dated from the early 1970s. Removing a floor created a double-height volume from which to regard one of the best views in Washington. Inside, a wall of books extends up three stories. On the exterior, teak sunshades protect the new steel and glass façade from the southern sun.

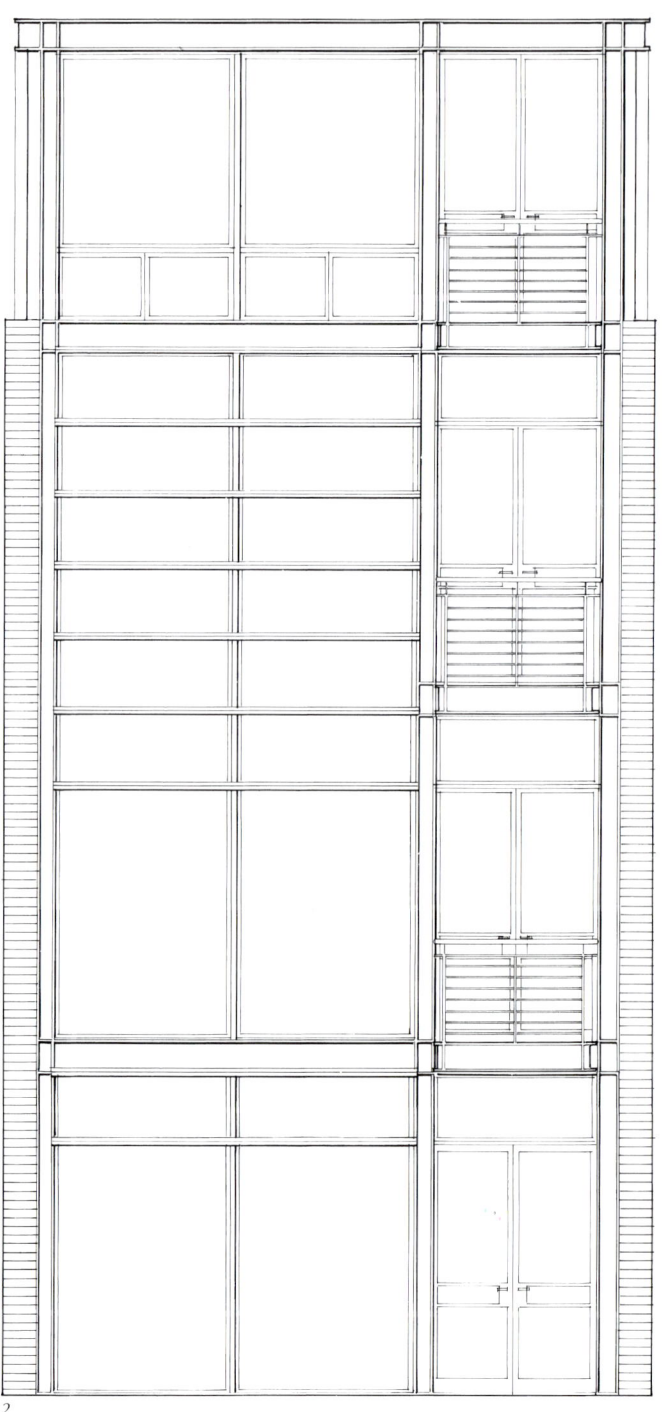

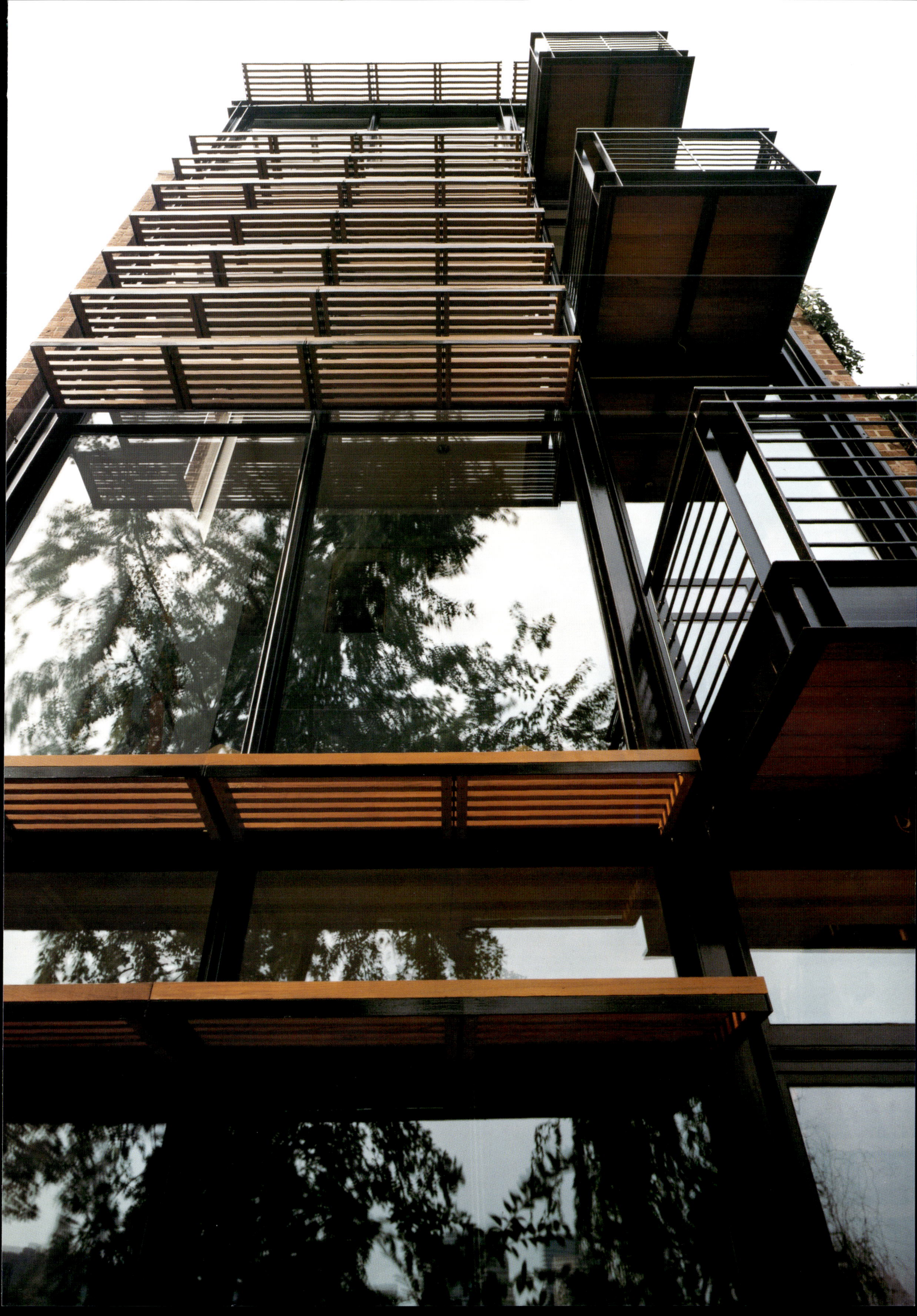

4 Dining room, with stairs up to view room
5 Section

5

McInturff Architects | 101

3rd floor

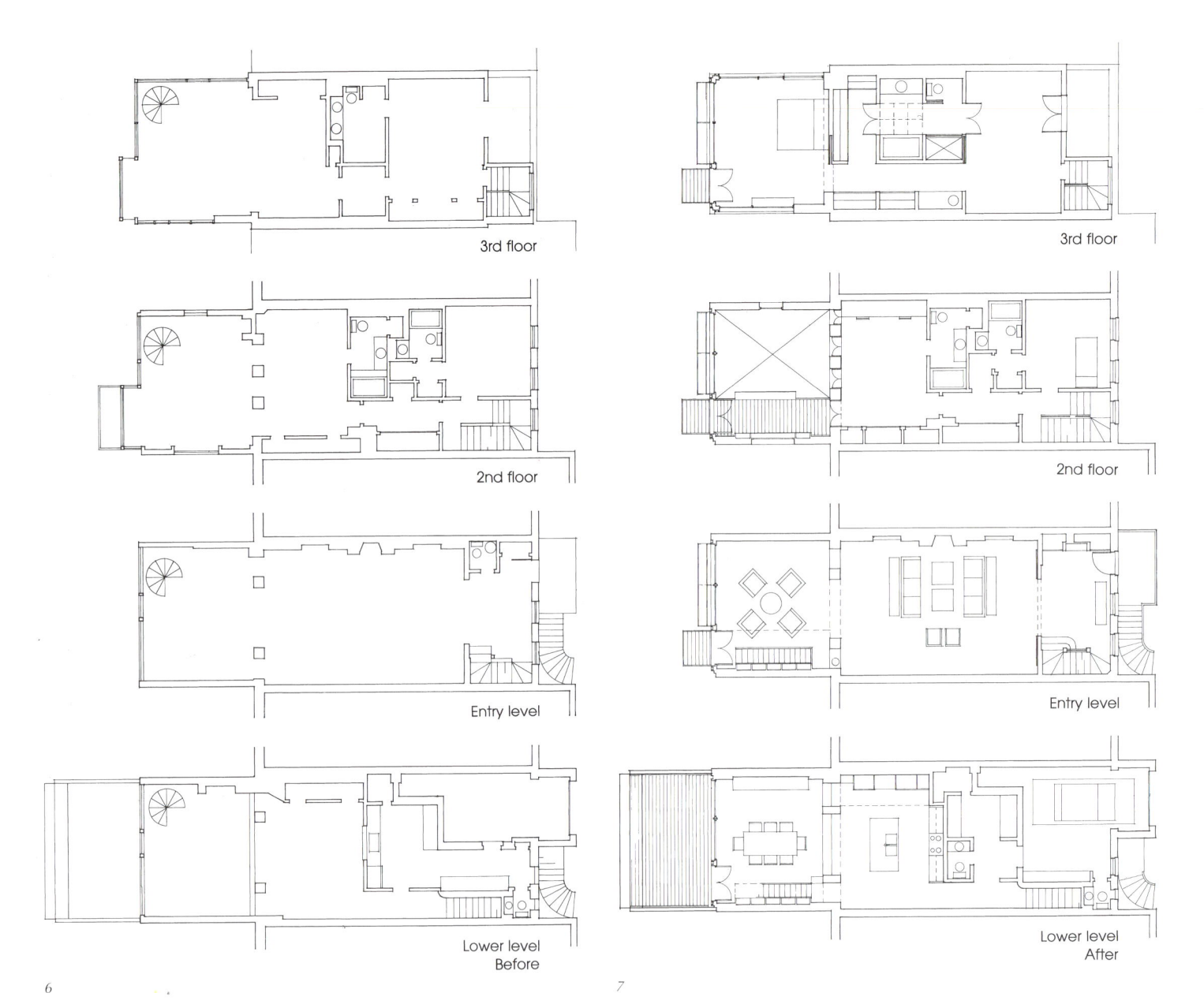

3rd floor

2nd floor

2nd floor

Entry level

Entry level

Lower level
Before

Lower level
After

6

7

6   Plans, before
7   Plans, after
8   Master bedroom
9   Model
10 Axonometric
11 Dining room with kitchen beyond

8

102 | COZZENS RESIDENCE

9

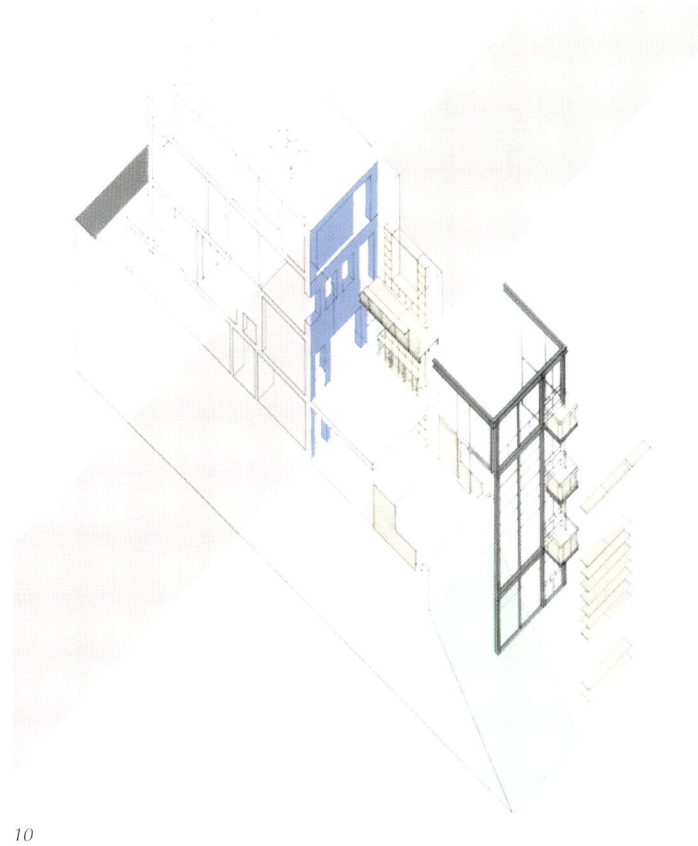

10

11

McInturff Architects | 103

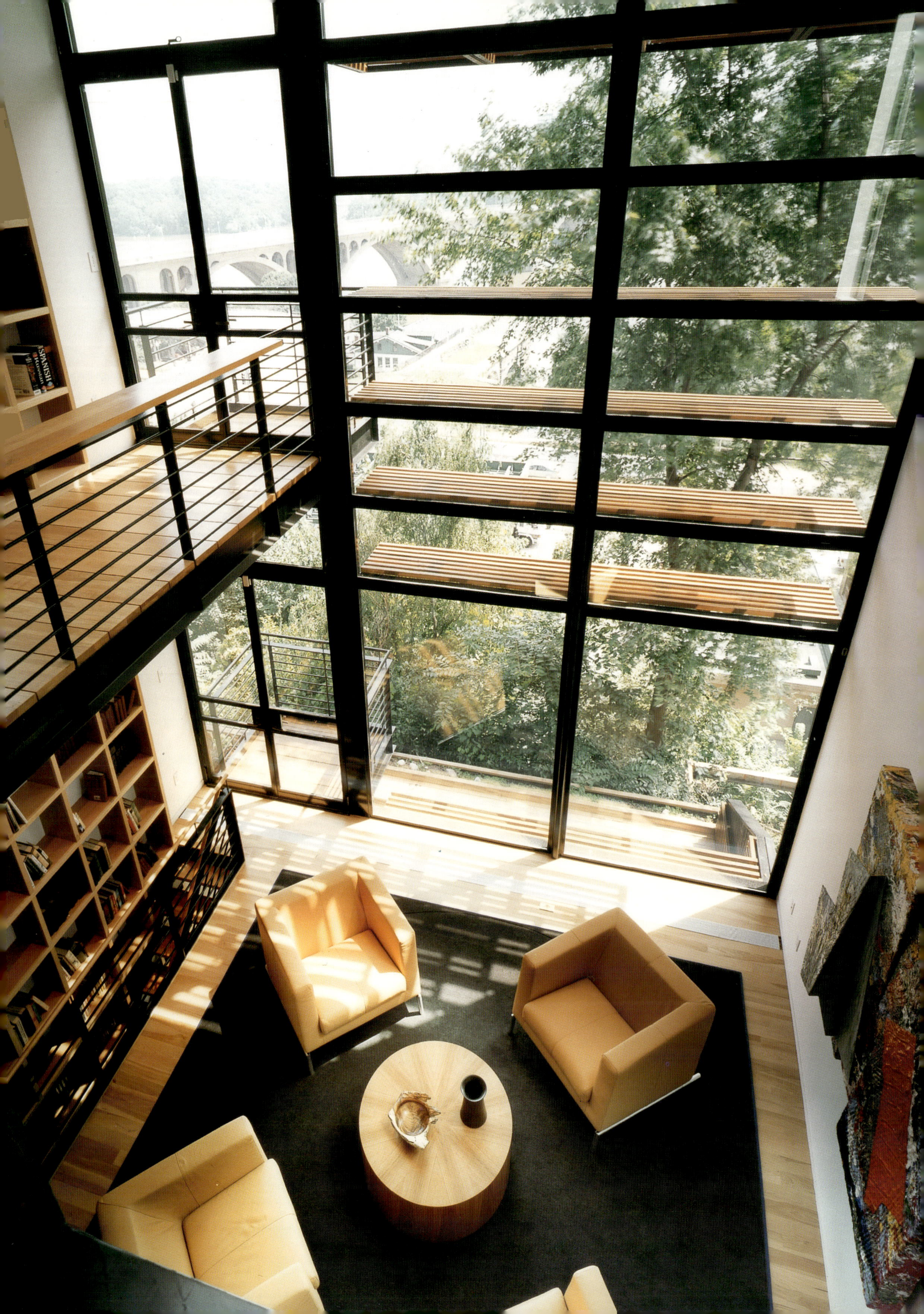
SPANISH

13

14

Opposite:
   Double-height view room and bridge from study
13   View room
14   View from study bridge

McInturff Architects | 105

MARTIN SHOCKET RESIDENCE

Chevy Chase, Maryland, USA
Completion: 2000

When our clients bought their 1920s foursquare catalog house in an older suburb of Washington DC, they discovered a one-story building of equal footprint in the backyard. Built as a commercial photographer's studio, but never used as such, it was detached from the house by a hyphen that resolved a half-story level change. Our job was to integrate this room into the life of house and family.

We did this by opening up the connection between the two volumes, and by giving the resulting family room a strong orientation to the wide side garden. A spare modern aesthetic contrasts happily with the existing house. Steel windows, glass block for privacy from neighbors, and a column-free porch accommodate the various orientations.

Given the generous dimensions of the room, it was possible to articulate walls and ceiling by projecting surface planes into the space without sacrificing function. Reveals between the planes have concealed lights and blinds. The room is furnished sparely, with a television behind rolling doors, a two-sided fireplace and a pool table. A cantilevered bench on a glass block wall invites repose while the owner runs the table.

1 Steel and glass canopy over porch
2 View from garden

McInturff Architects | 107

3

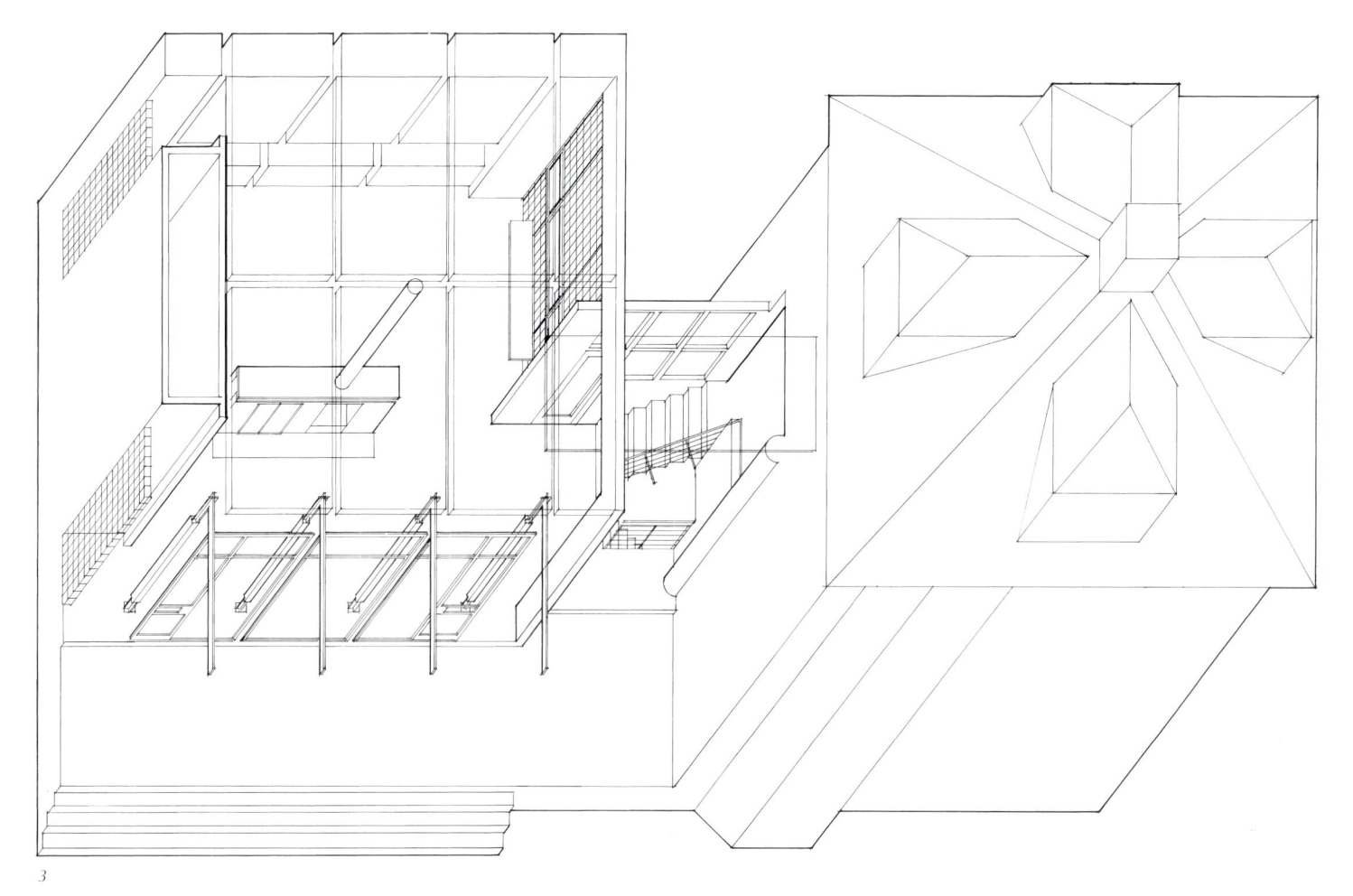

3 Axonometric
4 Two-sided fireplace with garden beyond
5 View of articulated wall and ceiling planes

4

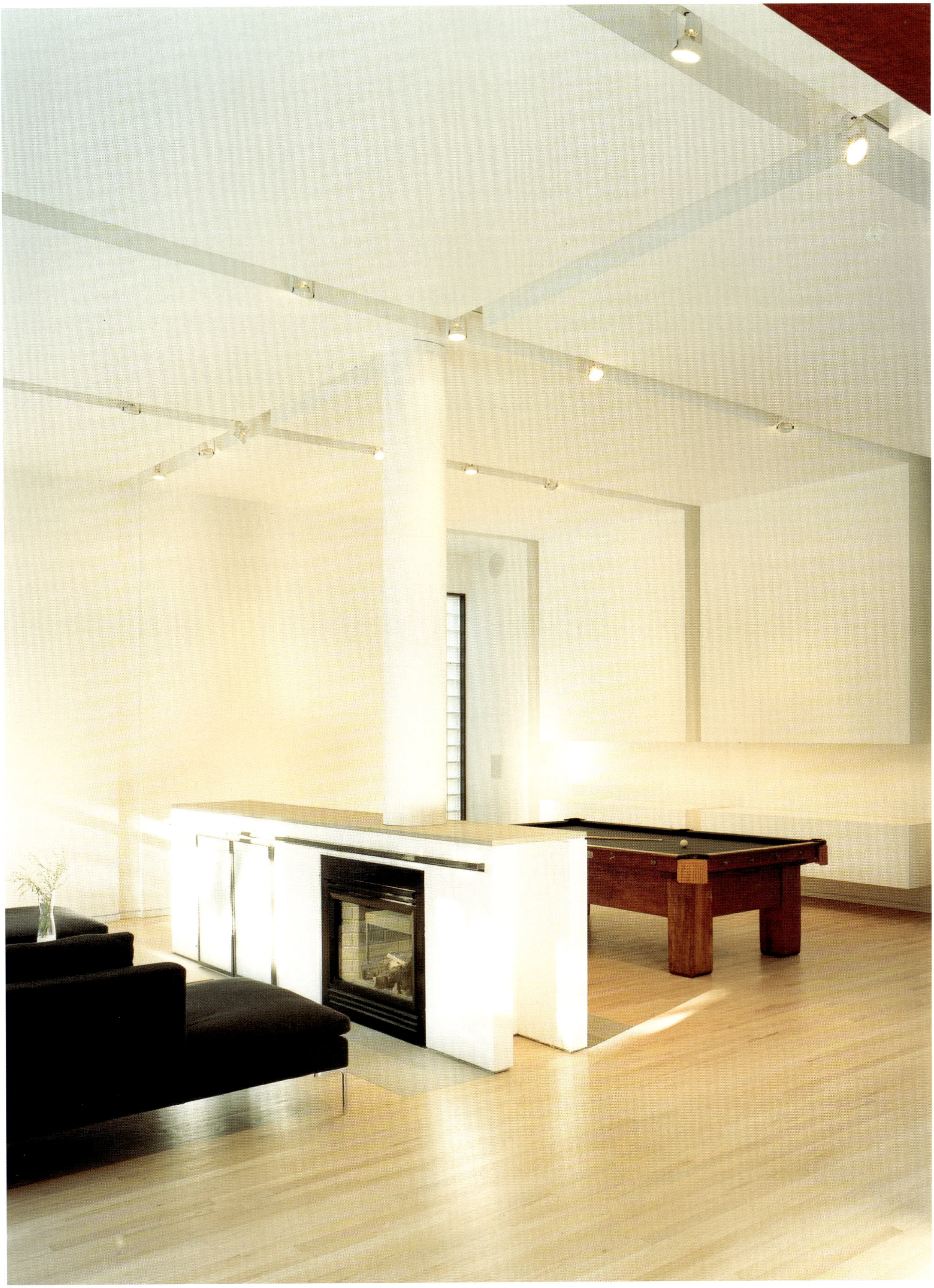

5

6 Seating area with fireplace and glass panels over television cabinet
7 Detail of interior screens and exterior steel and glass canopy
8 Site plan/plan, before
9 Family room

8

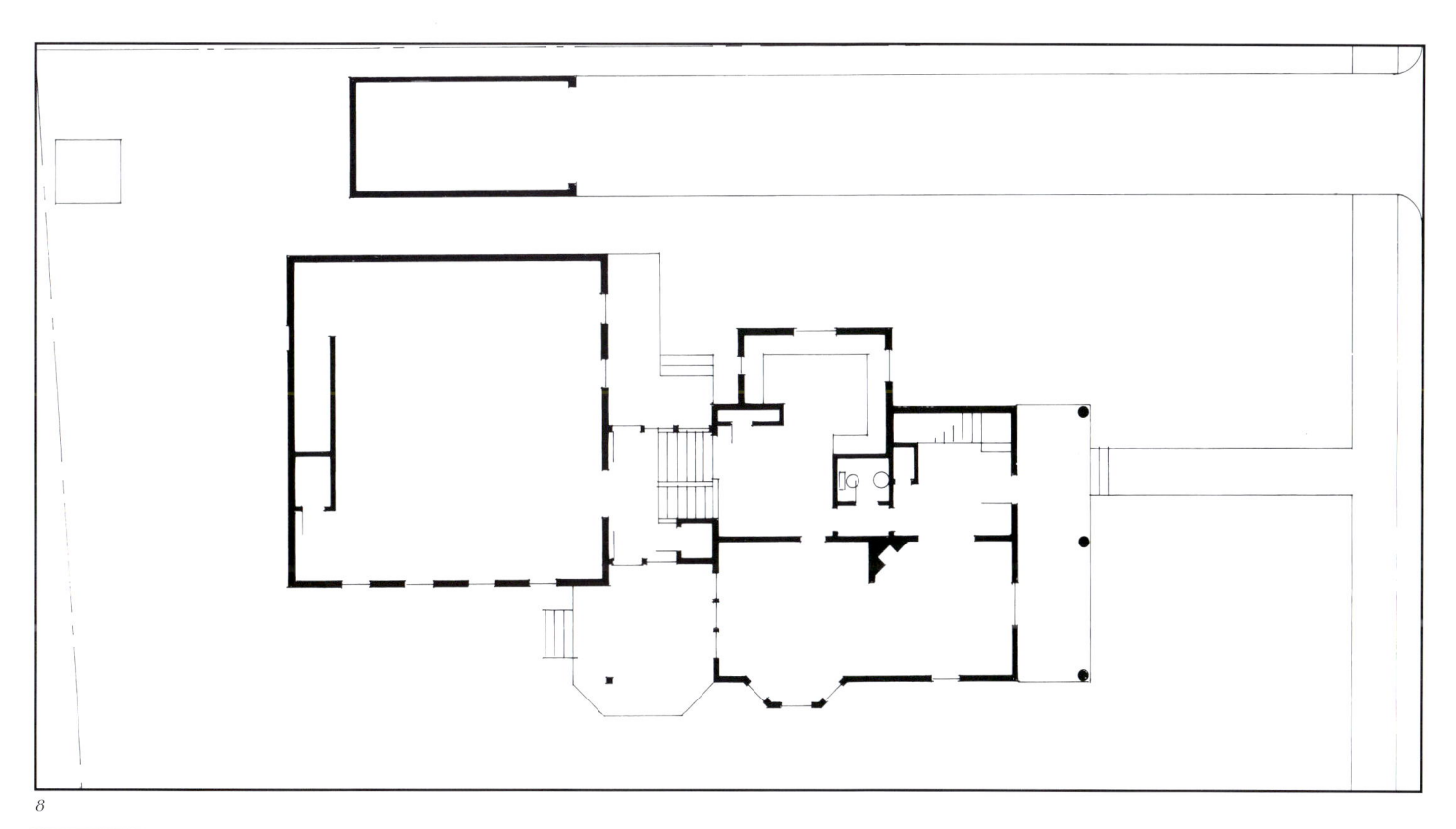

9

McInturff Architects | 111

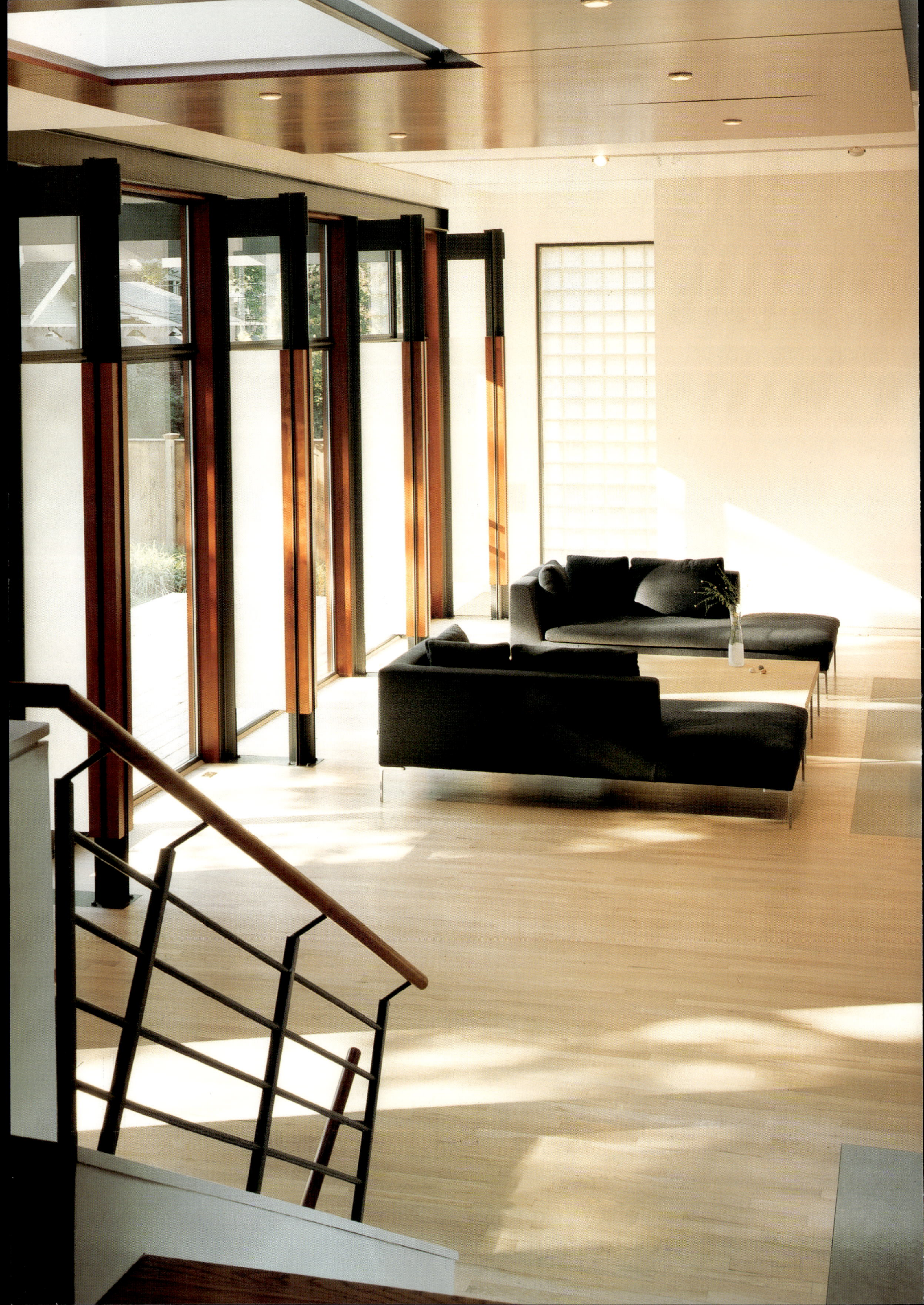

Opposite:
Family room from link to main house
11 Glass-block wall screens view of driveway beyond
12 Detail of cherry, steel and glass screens

SELECTED WORKS

MCINTURFF HOUSE + STUDIO
Bethesda, Maryland, USA
Completion: 1982–2000

It began as three run-down cottages in a then-neglected neighborhood near the Potomac River. The results—house, studio, gardens, pavilions, garages, pool, terraces—represent an ongoing 20-year effort.

The house began life as two small shacks. A stair now fills the narrow space between them, joining them into a single house. The third shack has become the studio, formalizing the integration of life and work. The collection of buildings form a kind of small village on the one-acre hillside site. It is intended that this will continue to change as time and energy permit.

Site axonometric

West façade (circa 1986)

JAKOB RESIDENCE
Washington DC, USA
Completion: 1989

The intention of this project was to maximize, with a minimum of means, the relationship of a modest 1930s rowhouse to adjacent urban parkland. We added a new room with a view of the park, and a second-floor roof deck for the owner and his cactus collection. Steel pipe columns and beams open the back wall and support the new roof deck above. There, the steel frame extends to support a vaulted structure covered with a mesh screen, shading the roof deck below.

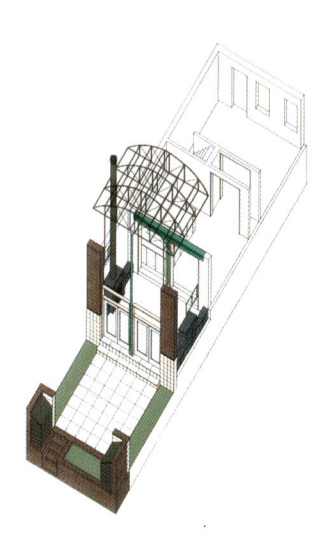

Axonometric

Exterior view

KNIGHT WEEKEND HOUSE
Front Royal, Virginia, USA
Completion: 1989

This tiny weekend house is in an open meadow that slopes to a river. It is a variation on a shotgun house, with the rooms lined up and stepping downhill toward the view. Wall colors and materials signify servant and served spaces, and bearing and nonbearing structure. All is gathered beneath the austere roof, a form derived from simply built agricultural buildings in the area. Homage to context may be lost on the locals, who call the house, with what one hopes is affection, 'the Gypsy caravan.'

TAYLOR RESIDENCE II
Washington DC, USA
Completion: 1991

The total renovation of a 19th century townhouse included the reconstruction of its original street façade. A fourth floor of living space was added by excavating the former basement, and the construction of a new rear façade added 4 feet of depth. The design of the existing floors has been developed with respect to their tradition, while the former basement—now kitchen and dining room—is seen as having a less restrictive aesthetic involving metal, stone, and stucco—a sort of 20th century cave.

Great room

Downhill elevation

Kitchen

Rail detail at rear window

SPRING VALLEY RESIDENCE
Washington DC, USA
Completion: 1991

By converting the typical American street-orientated living room to a kitchen, and orientating a new living room toward the garden, this house reasserts the primacy of private space, joining house and garden into an extended sequence. Throughout, spare detailing in natural materials—mahogany, granite, aluminum—has united the open plan. Space is interrupted, but not entirely divided, by screen walls, sliding panels, and an aluminum vault above the main seating, which reappears, in an abstracted form, on the rear façade.

FEFFER YINGLING BEACH HOUSE
Rehoboth Beach, Delaware, USA
Completion: 1992

This vacation house sits on a picturesque canal near the Atlantic Ocean, opening to westerly views of a wetland preserve. The canal façade breaks down into three pavilions (guests, owners, and shared) of graduated heights, unified by a continuous first-floor colonnade and deck. Everyone meets in the great room and a screened porch that serves as an interior courtyard—open air, yet protected from weather and mosquitoes. A post and beam structural system unites great room and porch, and differentiates them from simpler adjacent rooms.

Kitchen

Double-height screened porch

Garden façade

Canal façade

HARTH RESIDENCE
Bethesda, Maryland, USA
Completion: 1992

The interior renovation of a 1960s house has taken advantage of the original free plan and generous gabled section, while creating a needed hierarchy of space. Central, both to the rooms and to the idea of unifying/separating elements, is a large cabinet that faces each major area, becoming all things to all rooms—closet, kitchen storage, desk support, book shelves, bar, stereo cabinet, lighting, and display for art. It becomes, in many ways, the heart of the house, around which people, and space, revolve.

ANDREWS VIUDEZ RESIDENCE + STUDIO
Mount Rainier, Maryland, USA
Completion: 1993

This tiny project solves several problems through one carefully crafted insertion. A low-ceilinged attic became a light-filled painting studio, and some ungainly additions to this modest and once modestly charming cottage were brought under control.

A new clerestory light monitor reuses the structure of an old flat-center roof, supported by existing beams, new collar ties, timber corbels, and two log columns. The concentration of energy, structure, and cash to one critical point improved quality and quantity of space, while re-establishing the simple hierarchy of shapes that characterized the original cottage.

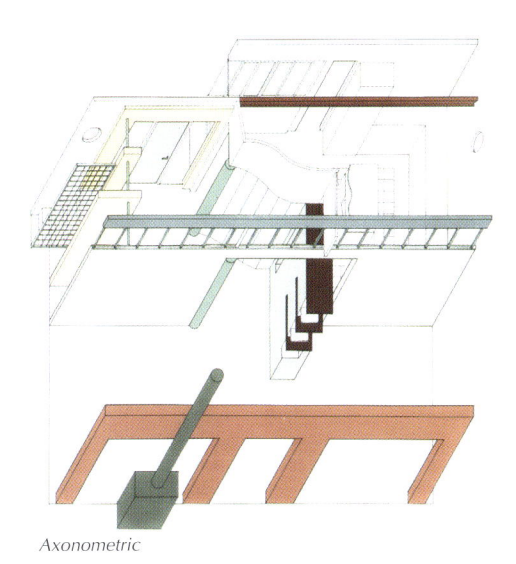

Axonometric

Garden elevation

Studio light monitor

View from entry

SIGMA NU FRATERNITY HOUSE
GEORGE WASHINGTON UNIVERSITY
Washington DC, USA
Completion: 1993

This house was collapsing around the brothers, who at the last minute rallied alumni support to fund a renovation. The rooms that retained vestiges of their original quality have been renovated. The basement became a new social room, in a new vocabulary. Old and new meet where a two-story bay window opens the social room to a new library above, which reinforces, or reintroduces, the idea of the coexistence of academic and social lives. On Saturday night, as the students dance below, there is always the reminder, from above, of the other reason for being here.

O'CONNOR BEACH HOUSE
Bethany Beach, Delaware, USA
Completion: 1996

This ample beach house accommodates an extended family of three generations. The plan is simple, with each floor a variation of the subdivision of a nine-square grid. A solid face is presented to the street, but the grid is carved away on the ocean side to maximize views. This also creates the most important space—a large deck, whose flanking towers frame the view and provide privacy from neighbors. Here, the family can congregate for a serene moment away from their busy worlds.

Rear elevation

Social room with library above

View from beach

Detail of deck tower

BARTLETT IGNANI RESIDENCE
Washington DC, USA
Completion: 1997

A three-story tower addition to a 1940s foursquare brick house was designed with a lightness of form, structure, and material that contrasts with the existing masonry house in a way that complements both. The new work is all about light.

The exterior skin is a grid of windows and glass wall panels, overhung with a delicate protective roof. The interior of the kitchen and family room is all light and reflection—porcelain tiles, maple cabinets, glass backsplashes, pale granite, and stainless steel counters.

BRONSTEIN COHEN LIBRARY
Washington DC, USA
Completion: 1998

The addition of a library to this 1908 Arts & Crafts house took over the precious side yard of the client, an avid gardener, so we decided to design the library as a garden room.

A stucco and stone octagon connects to the house by a highly fenestrated link that evokes a filled-in loggia. The library, 16 feet wide and 12 feet tall, is dipped in cherry up to the sills of the clerestories. During the day, lit from all sides, the wood gleams; at night it is like a beacon, glowing in the garden.

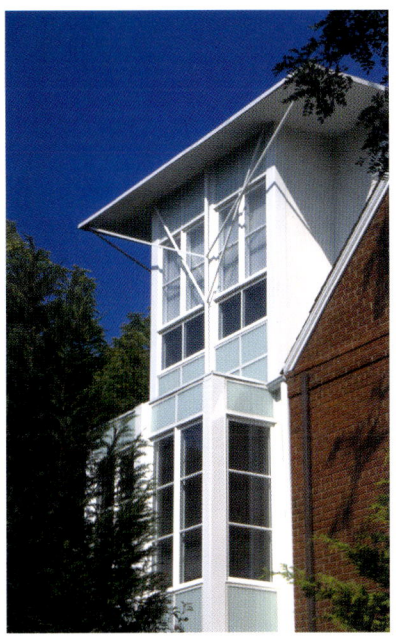

Tower detail

Library from new link to house

Kitchen

Library exterior

McInturff Architects

TASKER HOUSE
Rappahannock, Virginia
2000

This weekend house for our clients, their extended family and many guests commands a meadow site in the Virginia mountains. Through color, form and organization it abstractly recalls local rural building traditions.

APARTMENT HOUSE IN WASHINGTON DC
Schematic design 2000

This preliminary design for a new apartment building on the border of an historic neighborhood in Washington collages house-sized façades onto a nine-story structure. Within, a rotunda is carved away to form a courtyard which will provide a serene escape from urban life.

Entry courtyard

Model – Street façade

Detail of music room

Model – Rear façade

RAFF HOUSE
St. Michaels, Maryland

Situated on a waterfront bend on a Maryland river, this ample house for old friends is broken into several pieces, all straddling an axial approach beneath a tree canopy that recalls earlier Eastern shore precedents. Construction on the project is scheduled to begin in fall 2001.

ADDITION TO A VIRGINIA FARM
King George County, Virginia

This addition to an extraordinary moderne farmhouse (not, in itself, a common sight) extends its existing white-painted brick geometries and adds a louvered tower containing a porch and guestrooms. A courtyard is formed between new and old, directing the view to the river below. The project is scheduled for completion in 2002.

Model

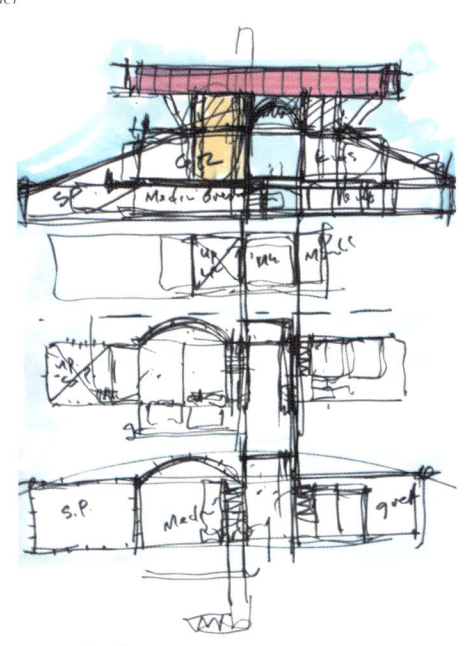

Model of new tower

Design sketch

Design sketch

FIRM PROFILE

McInturff Architects
McInturff Architects was formed in 1986 in a small hillside cottage that has grown over time to house the six-person firm with a diversified client base which includes residential, commercial and small institutional projects. It is the firm's assumption, and hope, that it is possible to make a viable, vital practice with an orientation toward the design of small, highly crafted projects. The architects are typically involved in the entire range of services, from project programming through complete architectural and interior design, utilizing a process with considerable client interaction and involvement in an effort to tailor buildings to the needs of their users. Our work has been frequently published, both locally and nationally, and the firm has received more than 150 design awards.

Mark McInturff
Mark McInturff FAIA is a native of Washington DC and received his Bachelor of Architecture from the University of Maryland School of Architecture with its first graduating class in 1972. He has taught at the University of Maryland since 1980, where he is currently an adjunct associate professor, and since 1995 has been a visiting critic at the Catholic University of America's School of Architecture and Planning. Mark McInturff was elevated to the College of Fellows of the AIA in 2000.

Architectural
Mark McInturff
Stephen Lawlor
Julia Heine
Peter Noonan
Christopher Boyd

Meghan Walsh
Caroline Sonner
Miche Booz
Julia Harrison
Tom Bucci
Norman Smith
Charles Lehner

Administrative
Catherine McInturff

Interns & Modelmakers
Gjergj Bakallbashi
Kevin Schiller

Nick Snyder
Aaron Wilch
Douglas Campbell
Jin Yong Kim
Edowa Shimizu

WORKS AND CREDITS

Addition to a Virginia Farm
Project Team: Mark McInturff, Stephen Lawlor
Contractor: Bonitt Builders

Andrews Viudez Studio + Residence
Project Team: Mark McInturff
Owners: David Andrews & Joanna Viudez
Contractors: David Andrews & Joanna Viudez
Garden Design: Joanna Viudez
Awards
- 1994 AIA/Maryland Society Citation
- 1993 AIA/Potomac Valley Citation

Armstrong House
Project Team: Mark McInturff, Peter Noonan
Owners: John & Linda Armstrong
Contractor: Bonin & Associates
Landscape Architect: Edward Alexander
Awards
- 1999 AIA/Potomac Valley Merit Award
- 2001 *Custom Home* Merit Award

Apartment House in Washington DC
Project Team: Mark McInturff, Stephen Lawlor
Owner: Furioso Development

Bartlett Ignani Residence
Project Team: Mark McInturff, Peter Noonan, Julia Heine
Owners: Larry Bartlett & Karen Ignani
Contractor: Acadia Contractors
Awards
- 1998 AIA/Potomac Valley Citation

Borsecnik Weil Residence
Project Team: Mark McInturff, Caroline Sonner, Julia Heine
Owners: Katherine Borsecnik & Gene Weil
Contractor: Acadia Contractors
Custom Woodwork: A. E. Boland
Awards
- 1998 AIA/Washington DC-*Washingtonian* Residential Design Award
- 1997 AIA/Baltimore-*Baltimore Magazine* Residential Design Award
- Renaissance '97 Merit Award
- 1996 AIA/Maryland Society Merit Award
- 1996 AIA/Potomac Valley Honor Award

Bronstein Cohen Library
Project Team: Mark McInturff, Julia Heine
Owners: Harriet Bronstein & Tom Cohen
Contractor: Roy Goertner
Custom Woodwork: Roy Goertner
Mason: PR Stone & Masonry
Awards
- 1999 AIA/Baltimore-*Baltimore Magazine* Residential Design Award
- Renaissance '99 Merit Award
- 1998 AIA/Maryland Society Merit Award
- 1998 AIA/Potomac Valley Merit Award

Couch Weekend House
Project Team: Mark McInturff, Miche Booz
Owner: Jane Couch
Contractor: Bruce Behrens
Awards
- 2000 AIA/Washington DC Merit Award in Architecture
- 1996 AIA/Maryland Society Honor Award
- 1996 AIA/Baltimore-*Baltimore Magazine* Residential Design Award
- 1995 AIA/Potomac Valley Honor Award
- 1995 AIA/Washington DC-*Washingtonian* Residential Design Award
- 1995 *Custom Home* Merit Award
- 1995 Builder's Choice Merit Award

Cozzens Residence
Project Team: Mark McInturff, Julia Heine
Owner: Todd Cozzens
Contractor: Acadia Contractors
Custom Woodwork: A. E. Boland
Steelwork: ABC Welding
Artwork: Hemphill Fine Arts
Awards
- 2000 AIA/Maryland Society Merit Award
- 2000 AIA/Potomac Valley Merit Award

Denning Residence
Project Team: Mark McInturff
Owner: Jacqueline Denning
Contractor: Shorieh Talaat Design Associates
Awards
- 1993 AIA/Maryland Society Merit Award
- 1992 AIA/Virginia Society *Inform* Honor Award
- 1992 AIA/Washington DC Merit Award in Interior Architecture
- 1992 AIA/Washington DC-*Washingtonian* Residential Design Award
- Renaissance '92 Merit Award
- 1991 AIA/Potomac Valley Honor Award

Feffer Yingling Beach House
Project Team: Mark McInturff, Stephen Lawlor
Owners: Gerald Feffer & Monique Yingling
Contractor: Bradley Construction
Awards
- 1994 AIA/Washington DC-*Washingtonian* Residential Design Award
- 1993 AIA/Maryland Society Honor Award
- 1993 Builder's Choice Merit Award
- 1992 AIA/Potomac Valley Honor Award

Feller Residence
Project Team: Mark McInturff, Peter Noonan
Owner: Mimi Feller
Contractor: Acadia Contractors
Awards
- 2000 AIA/Virginia Society *Inform* Award
- 1999 *Custom Home* Merit Award
- Renaissance '97 Grand Award
- 1996 AIA/Washington DC Award of Excellence in Architecture
- 1996 AIA/Washington DC-*Washingtonian* Residential Design Award
- 1996 AIA/Baltimore-*Baltimore Magazine* Residential Design Award
- 1996 AIA/Maryland Society Honor Award
- 1995 AIA/Potomac Valley Citation

Hanson Sciannella Residence
Project Team: Mark McInturff, Peter Noonan
Owners: Roberta Hanson & Frank Sciannella
Contractor: Dreieck Builders Group
Custom Woodwork: A. E. Boland
Interior Design: Michael Foster
Awards
- 2000 AIA/Virginia Society *Inform* Award
- *residential architect* Design 2000 Merit Award
- 2000 *Custom Home* Grand Award
- Renaissance 2000 Project of the Year
- 2000 Builder's Choice Special Focus Award
- 1999 AIA/Maryland Society Honor Award
- 1999 AIA/Washington DC Award of Excellence in Interior Architecture
- 1999 AIA/Baltimore-*Baltimore Magazine* Residential Design Award
- 1999 AIA/Potomac Valley Merit Award

Harth Residence
Project Team: Mark McInturff, Miche Booz
Owners: Alberto & Nadine Harth
Contractor: Upright Construction
Awards
- 1993 AIA/Maryland Society Merit Award
- 1993 AIA/Washington DC-*Washingtonian* Residential Design Award
- 1992 AIA/Potomac Valley Merit Award

Heard Teng Residence II
Project Team: Mark McInturff, Julia Heine
Owners: Lane Heard & Mei Su Teng
Contractor: Roy Goertner
Mason: PR Stone & Masonry
Steelwork: Diamond Welding, Dameron Forge
Awards
- 1999 *Custom Home* Merit Award
- Renaissance '99 Grand Award
- 1998 AIA/Maryland Society Merit Award
- 1998 AIA/Virginia Society *Inform* Award
- 1998 AIA/Potomac Valley Honor Award
- 1998 AIA/Baltimore-*Baltimore Magazine* Residential Design Award

House in the Woods
Project Team: Mark McInturff, Peter Noonan
Contractor: Frontier Construction
Interior Design: Susan Agger
Landscape Architect: Lila Fendrick
Awards
- 1998 AIA/Potomac Valley Honor Award

Hutner Residence
Project Team: Mark McInturff, Peter Noonan, Julia Heine
Owners: David & Susan Hutner
Contractor: Acadia Contractors
Awards
- 1996 AIA/Maryland Society Merit Award
- 1997 AIA/Baltimore-*Baltimore Magazine* Residential Design Award
- 1996 *Custom Home* Merit Award
- 1996 Builder's Choice Merit Award
- Renaissance '96 Merit Award
- 1995 AIA/Potomac Valley Merit Award

Jakob Residence
Project Team: Mark McInturff, Tom Bucci, Norman Smith, Charles Lehner
Owner: Felix Jakob
Contractor: Lamont Green
Steelwork: Dameron Forge
Awards
- 1991 AIA/Maryland Society Merit Award
- 1991 AIA/Washington DC Award of Excellence in Architecture
- 1990 AIA/Washington DC-*Washingtonian* Residential Design Award
- Renaissance '90 Merit Award
- 1989 AIA/Potomac Valley Honor Award

King Residence
Project Team: Mark McInturff, Miche Booz
Owners: Charles & Diane King
Contractor: Acadia Contractors
Awards
- 1998 AIA/Virginia Society *Inform* Award
- 1995 AIA/Maryland Society Merit Award
- 1995 Builder's Choice Merit Award
- Renaissance '95 Project of the Year
- 1994 AIA/Potomac Valley Merit Award

Knight House III
Project Team: Mark McInturff, Peter Noonan, Julia Heine
Owners: Jonathan & Judith Knight
Contractor: Acadia Contractors
Custom Woodwork: A. E. Boland
Awards
- 1998 AIA/Washington DC-*Washingtonian* Residential Design Award
- 1995 AIA/Maryland Society Merit Award
- 1995 AIA/Virginia Society *Inform* Merit Award
- 1995 AIA/Potomac Valley Merit Award

Knight Weekend House
Project Team: Mark McInturff, Norman Smith, Tom Bucci, Julia Heine
Owners: Jonathan & Judith Knight
Contractor: Douglas Thomas Construction
Awards
- 1993 AIA/Washington DC-*Washingtonian* Residential Design Award
- 1991 AIA/Maryland Society Honor Award
- 1991 American Wood Council Honor Award
- 1990 Builder's Choice Grand Award
- 1989 AIA/Potomac Valley Honor Award

Martin Shocket Residence
Project Team: Mark McInturff, Peter Noonan
Owners: Patricia Martin & David Shocket
Contractor: Acadia Contractors
Awards
- 2000 AIA/Maryland Society Merit Award
- 2000 AIA/Washington DC Award of Excellence in Interior Architecture
- 2000 AIA/Potomac Valley Citation

McInturff House + Studio
Project Team: Mark McInturff
Owners: Catherine & Mark McInturff
Contractor: Mark McInturff
Awards
- Renaissance '90 Merit Award
- 1988 AIA/Potomac Valley Merit Award
- 1987 Builder's Choice Awards
- 1986 American Wood Council Merit Award

O'Connor Beach House
Project Team: Mark McInturff, Peter Noonan, Eve Murty
Owners: Pamela & Kevney O'Connor
Contractor: Boardwalk Builders
Awards
- 1999 AIA/Maryland Society Honor Award
- 1999 AIA/Potomac Valley Citation

Private Residence
Project Team: Mark McInturff, Miche Booz
Contractor: Lofgren Construction
Awards
- 1995 AIA/Washington DC-*Washingtonian* Residential Design Award
- 1994 AIA/Maryland Society Citation
- 1994 AIA/Washington DC Merit Award in Architecture
- 1994 Builder's Choice Special Focus Award
- 1993 AIA/Potomac Valley Honor Award
- Renaissance '93 Grand Award

Raff House
Project Team: Mark McInturff, Peter Noonan, Chris Boyd
Owners: Dee & Mel Raff
Contractor: Ilex Construction

Residence in Old Town
Project Team: Mark McInturff, Stephen Lawlor
Contractor: Bonitt Builders
Custom Woodwork: A. E. Boland
Awards
- 2000 AIA/Maryland Society Honor Award
- 1999 AIA/Potomac Valley Merit Award

Sigma Nu Fraternity House
Project Team: Mark McInturff, Stephen Lawlor
Owners: Sigma Nu Fraternity, Delta Pi Chapter, George Washington University
Contractor: Hodgson Builders
Awards
- 1994 AIA/Potomac Valley Citation
- 1994 Builder's Choice Merit Award
- 1993 AIA/Maryland Society Honor Award

Spring Valley Residence
Project Team: Mark McInturff, Miche Booz
Contractor: Hodgson Builders
Awards
- 1993 Builder's Choice Merit Award
- 1992 AIA/Virginia Society *Inform* Merit Award
- 1991 AIA/Washington DC Merit Award in Architecture
- 1991 AIA/Potomac Valley Honor Award

Tasker House
Project Team: Mark McInturff, Stephen Lawlor
Owners: Connie & Joe Tasker
Contractor: Rappahannock Design & Building Company
Custom Millwork: Bob Lucking

Taylor Residence II
Project Team: Mark McInturff, Miche Booz, Julia Heine
Owners: Bonnie & David Taylor
Contractor: Heirman Renovations
Awards
- 1992 AIA/Virginia Society *Inform* Merit Award
- 1992 AIA/Washington DC-*Washingtonian* Residential Design Award
- 1991 AIA/Maryland Society Citation
- 1990 AIA/Potomac Valley Merit Award

Weiner Residence II
Project Team: Mark McInturff, Peter Noonan
Owner: David Weiner
Contractor: Renovations Unlimited
Awards
- 2000 AIA/Washington DC-*Washingtonian* Residential Design Award
- *residential architect* Design 2000 Merit Award
- Renaissance 2000 Grand Award

Withers House
Project Team: Mark McInturff, Stephen Lawlor
Owner: Josephine Withers
Contractor: Joe Barry
Artist: Janet Saad Cook
Awards
- *residential architect* Design 2000 Project of the Year,
- 1999 AIA/Maryland Society Merit Award
- 1999 AIA/Virginia Society *Inform* Award
- 1999 AIA/Washington DC Award of Excellence in Architecture
- 1999 AIA/Washington DC-*Washingtonian* Residential Design Award
- 1999 AIA/Baltimore-*Baltimore Magazine* Residential Design Award
- 1999 *Custom Home* Project of the Year,
- 1999 Builder's Choice Grand Award
- 1998 AIA/Potomac Valley Merit Award

SELECTED BIBLIOGRAPHY

Abramson, Susan and Stuchin, Marcie. *Bedrooms & Private Spaces: Designer Dreamscapes*, "Attic Suite," (PBC International 1997). pp. 44–47.

Abramson, Susan & Stuchin, Marcie. *Waterside Homes*, "Maine Attraction," (PBC International 1998). pp. 156–159.

Book, Jeff. "Playing Against Type," *House Beautiful*, September 1997, p. 70.

"Break from the Past," *Home*, May 2000, pp. 116–123, cover.

"Bright & Airy: Open Up the Back," *House Beautiful Home Remodeling & Decorating*, Spring 1994, pp. 52–57.

Brophy, Mary and Silverstein, Wendy. "The Long and Narrow," *Home*, April 1988.

Clagett, Leslie. "Simply for Dining," *Home*, March 1990, pp. 107–108.

Clark, Sally. *Color*, "Reinventing the Modernist Canvas," House Beautiful Great Style Series (Hearst Books 1993), pp. 64–69.

"Classic & Contemporary," *Home*, October 1998, pp. 186–187.

Conroy, Claire and Ensor, Leslie. "The Best!" *Custom Home*, March/April 1999, pp. 77–81, 88–91, 102–103.

Copestick, Joanna. *The Family Home* (Stewart Tabori & Chang 1998). pp. 94

Day, Rebecca. "High Wired Acts," *Custom Home*, May 2000, pp. 62–65.

Deffenbagh, Paul and Moriarty, Anne Marie. "Renaissance '95—Best of the Year," *Remodeling*, November 1995, pp. 94–97.

Dermansky, Ann. "Before & After: Surviving the Space Race," *American HomeStyle*, October 1994, pp. 36–38.

Dickinson, Duo. *Small Houses for the Next Century, 2nd ed.* "Sacred Centerline" (McGraw Hill 1995) pp. 72–77.

Dietsch, Deborah K. "Dream Houses, Real-Life Budgets," *Washington Post*, 15 July 2000, pp. G1, G4–G6.

Dietsch, Deborah K. "Dream Houses: What's Going on Back There?," *Washington Post*, 30 March 2000, p. H7.

Drueding, Meghan. "In the Spotlight," *residential architect*, May/June 1998, pp. 68–69.

Drueding, Meghan. "*residential architect* 2000 Project of the Year," *residential architect*, May 2000, pp. 46–49, cover.

Edelson, Harriet. "Rehoboth Modern," *Washington Post*, 22 July 1993.

Forgey, Benjamin. "Cityscape: Starmaking Machinery," *Washington Post*, 16 August 2000, p. C5.

Forgey, Benjamin. "Standouts that Blend Right In," *Washington Post*, 24 August 1991.

Futagawa, Yukio. *GA Houses #11*, "Two Houses by Mark McInturff" (Global Architecture 1982).

Gelfeld, Elizabeth. "A Tower Looking at the View," *Washington Post*, 15 October 1998.

Geran, Monica. "Mark McInturff," *Interior Design*, February 1995, pp. 118–123.

"Getting It Wright," *Home*, May 1998, pp. 168–172.

Giovannini, Joseph. "Design Notebook: That Fickle Lover in Design Affairs," *The New York Times*, 25 November 1999, p. D4.

Granat, Diane. "Dream House," *Washingtonian*, October 1998.

"The Great Divide," *Home*, April 1997, pp. 128–133.

Hallam, Linda. "Liberated by the Hallway," *Southern Living*, February 1992, pp. 70–71.

"Hardwood Applications," *Asian Furniture News*, September 1996, pp. 88–89, 93.

"Heaven Sent," *American HomeStyle Kitchen & Bath Planner*, Summer 1994, pp. 66–68.

Herbers, Jill. *Great Adaptations* (Whitney Library of Design/Watson-Guptill Publications 1990) pp. 122–127.

Herbst, Robin. "House Proud: Conquering the Quirks of a Basement," *New York Times*, 3 March 1994, p. C4.

Herbst, Robin. "House Proud: Creative Ways for Inside Living to Drift Outside," *New York Times*, 9 June 1994, p. C4.

"It All Adds Up," *Home*, June 1998, pp. 137–143.

King, Carol Soucek. *Designing With Light: The Creative Touch*, "Material Transformation" (PBC International 1997) pp. 114–117

Kousoulas, George and Claudia. *Contemporary Architecture in Washington DC*, "Knight House," (The Preservation Press/National Trust For Historic Preservation, 1995) p. 303.

Kirchner, Jill. "A House for All Ages," *American HomeStyle & Gardening*, November 1998, pp. 85–91.

Kirchner, Jill. "Suite Retreats," *American HomeStyle & Gardening*, June 1998, pp. 66–67.

Landecker, Heidi. "Industrial Evolution," *Architecture*, April 1991, pp. 88–91.

Lobdell, Heather. "Welcoming Walls," *Better Homes & Gardens Bedroom & Bath*, Fall 1997, pp. 82–87.

McInturff, Mark. "Weiner Residence: Simple Wood Forms Make a Case for Understatement," *Wood Design & Building*, Spring 2000, pp. 18–21.

McInturff, Mark. 'When Home is the Office," *Custom Home*, July/August 1995, pp. 48–51.

McKee, Bradford. "Tectonic Steps," *Architecture*, March 1996, pp. 141–143.

Maviglio, Steven. "The Porch and How it Grew," *Decorating Remodeling*, June/July 1992, pp. 20–21.

Mays, Vernon. "McInturff Scores a Clean," *Inform*, Spring/Summer 1992, pp. 28–31.

"Modern Living," *Home*, May 2000, pp. 150–155.

"More Living Room," *Home*, March 1999, pp. 86–89, cover.

Nadel, Barbara A., FAIA. "Old Town's New Home," *Inland Architect*, volume 117 no.1, pp. 38–43.

Nesmith, Lynn. "Casual in the Capital," *Southern Living*, June 1995, pp. 140–142.

"Open Minded," *Home*, October 2000, pp. 144–155.

Patel, Nina, Powell, William, and Schuller, Joesph. "Renaissance 2000: Best of the Year," *Remodeling*, September 2000, pp. 44–47.

Perschetz, Lois. "Best Houses of '96," *Baltimore Magazine*, October 1996, pp. 82–87.

Pretzer, Michael. "Split Level Decisions," *Regardie's/Luxury Home Washington*, October/November 1991, pp. 104–107.

"Pure & Simple," *Custom Home*, March/April 1995, pp. 52–55.

"Rethinking the Dining Room," *Home*, November 1996, 138–139, cover.

Rogers, Patricia Dane. "American Original," *Washington Post*, 3 October 1996.

Rogers, Patricia Dane. "Designed to Click in Every Room in the House," *Washington Post*, 18 May 2000, p. H1.

Rogers, Patricia Dane. "Hang It All," *Washington Post*, 6 April 2000, p. H4.

Rogers, Patricia Dane. "Tradition with a Twist at the Delaware Shore," *Washington Post*, 31 July 2000.

Rosch, Leah. "River Light," *Metropolitan Home*, July/August 1996, pp. 84–87.

Seerich-Caldwell, Anja. *Starter Hauser*, (Karl Kramer Verlag 1998) pp. 118–121.

Sheehan, Carol Sama. *Kitchens*, House Beautiful Great Style Series (Hearst Books 1993) pp. 16, 64.

"Sleekness and Light," *Home*, March 2000, pp. 96–105, cover.

Smith-Morant, Deborah and Wilhide, Elizabeth. *Terence Conran's Kitchen Book* (Overlook Press, 1993) p. 187.

Smith, Norman. *Small Space Living* (Rockport Publishers/AIA Press 1995) pp. 13, 17, 20.

Stipe, Suzanne E. "A Simple Plan," *Baltimore Magazine*, October 1999, pp. 70–75.

"Thoroughly Modern," *Home*, February 1997, pp. 90–97, cover.

Vandervanter, Peter. "Minimalist Effort, " *Regardie's*, October 1990, pp. 38–41

Ward, Timothy J. "Local Hero," *Metropolitan Home*, October 1988, pp. 116–121, cover.

Weber, Cheryl. "Into the Light," *Remodeling*, October 1998, pp. 72–79.

"Well Crafted Kitchens," *Home*, September 1994, pp. 118–119.

Zevon, Susan. "Wood, Stone & Willpower," *House Beautiful*, July 1998, pp. 110–115.

ACKNOWLEDGMENTS

I believe in the small office—an office where it is possible to maintain a clear focus and coherent vision, an office where everyone does everything. We have kept our office small by intent and will continue to do so by design. I can think of few architects whose works improve as office size increases.

I believe there is a virtue in working with a small group of people over time, in developing an internal shorthand that only comes from continuous interaction. I am fortunate to have a group of people who have worked with me for a number of years and who each share credit for the work illustrated here. Stephen Lawlor, Julia Heine and Peter Noonan were all once my students at the University of Maryland, and we have grown together. In addition, Julia Heine deserves credit for the photography in this book. Finally, I am indebted to my wife Catherine, who, as office manager, endeavors to keep us solvent and legal.

I believe in the importance of the architect's role in the making of buildings and in the importance of the people who do the making. We are entirely indebted to the innumerable contractors and craftspeople who execute our work and, in many cases, help us to evolve our own understanding of our craft. They are too numerous to list here, but are well represented in the project credits. Special thanks to Neubauer Consulting Engineers, and, especially, to the unflappable Robert, for their contributions to our projects.

Finally, I am indebted to our clients who are frequently asked to make a leap of faith and, to my constant surprise and appreciation, do it.

Mark McInturff FAIA
Bethesda, Maryland
2001

INDEX

Addition to Virginia Farm	121, 124	Jakob Residence	114, 125
Andrews Viudez Studio + Residence	117, 124	King Residence	20, 125
Apartment House in Washington DC	120, 124	Knight House III	22, 125
Armstrong House	64, 124	Knight Weekend House	115, 125
Bartlett Ignani Residence	119, 124	Martin Shocket Residence	106, 125
Borsecnik Weil Residence	46, 124	McInturff House + Studio	114, 125
Bronstein Cohen Library	119, 124	O'Connor Beach House	118, 125
Couch Weekend House	30, 124	Private Residence	12, 125
Cozzens Residence	98, 124	Raff House	121, 125
Denning Residence	8, 124	Residence in Old Town	72, 125
Feffer Yingling Beach House	116, 124	Sigma Nu Fraternity House	118, 125
Feller Residence	38, 124	Spring Valley Residence	116, 125
Hanson Sciannella Residence	80, 124	Tasker House	120, 125
Harth Residence	117, 124	Taylor Residence II	115, 125
Heard Teng Residence II	58, 124	Weiner Residence II	86, 125
House in the Woods	52, 124	Withers House	92, 125
Hutner Residence	42, 124		